# COMPOSITE BOWS
# FROM THE TOMB OF
# TUT'ANKHAMŪN

TUT'ANKHAMŪN'S TOMB SERIES

*General Editor:* J. R. HARRIS

III

# COMPOSITE BOWS FROM THE TOMB OF TUT'ANKHAMŪN

BY

W. McLEOD

OXFORD

PRINTED FOR THE GRIFFITH INSTITUTE
AT THE UNIVERSITY PRESS
BY VIVIAN RIDLER
1970

PRINTED IN GREAT BRITAIN

# ACKNOWLEDGEMENTS

To the Committee of Management of the Griffith Institute for permission to use Howard Carter's notes; to the staff and members of the Institute, particularly R. W. Hamilton, Rosalind L. B. Moss, Helen V. Murray, and Barbara M. Sewell, for their unstinting assistance to an absentee researcher; to Nora Scott, Associate Curator of the Department of Egyptian Art in the Metropolitan Museum of Art, for identification of Mace's handwriting, and for details about Burton's photographs; to J. F. Hughes, of the Commonwealth Forestry Institute, Oxford, for communicating data from the Institute's files; to Victor Girgis, First Curator of the Egyptian Museum in Cairo, for his hospitality to me on 3 January 1959; to Mohammad Hassan Abdul Rahman, Director of the Egyptian Museum, for his many courtesies to Miss Turzynski during her visits in 1966–7; to Eugene Robinson, of Napa, California, for sharing his notes and photographs from Cairo; to Robert A. Elder of the Office of Anthropology of the United States National Museum (Smithsonian Institution), John Lowry of the Indian Section of the Victoria and Albert Museum, and R. H. Pinder-Wilson of the Department of Oriental Antiquities of the British Museum, for providing information about objects in the collections of their respective Museums; to J. J. Balatinecz, S. Dow, M. B. Emeneau, C. S. Hanes, Winifred Needler, Lt.-Cdr. W. F. Paterson, and J. R. Wiggins, for guidance in various matters; to the Office of Research Administration of the University of Toronto for a grant to facilitate Miss Turzynski's researches and to purchase photographs; to the editors of the *American Journal of Archaeology*, the *Journal of the Society of Archer-Antiquaries*, and *Phoenix*, for permission to use material which appeared originally in the pages of these journals.

D. B. Redford prepared the translation of the inscriptions, and an initial commentary on them. B. Turzynski compared Carter's descriptions with the bows in Cairo, confirmed some identifications, provided other new ones, and added many details of decoration. At the request of the Editor—who here acknowledges his indebtedness— G. T. Martin collated as much as was possible of the inscriptions, correcting a number of readings, and making invaluable notes on the usurpation of the 'Bow of Honour'. The elegant hieroglyphs of the Plates are the work of A. H. Lenman, whose sudden death was a sad loss to future Egyptology. The final responsibility for the texts rests with the Editor.[1]

[1] The readings suggested by the original copies were sometimes suspect, but could in most cases be checked: a very few points remain in doubt. Where groups of signs, initially certain, have now flaked away (as, for example, in Inscriptions 6. 2 [*pḏt 9, mi rꜥ ḏt*], 11. 2 [*s₃ rꜥ*], 13. 2 [*sḫm*]) the inscription is shown as it was at the time of discovery. [Ed.]

NOTE

This catalogue supersedes the one included in my thesis, *The Bow in Ancient Greece* (Harvard, 1966), which preceded B. Turzynski's autopsy.

# CONTENTS

# LIST OF ABBREVIATIONS

The titles of journals are abbreviated in accordance with the list given in the *American Journal of Archaeology*, 69 (1965), pp. 201–6.

Bonnet, *Waffen* = H. Bonnet, *Die Waffen der Völker des alten Orients*, Leipzig, 1926.

CARTER–MACE = H. Carter and A. C. Mace, *The Tomb of Tut·ankh·Amen*, 3 vols., London, 1923–33. (The pagination is different in the New York edition.)

*Eg. Ornament* = P. Fořtová-Šámalová and M. Vilímková, *Egyptian Ornament*, London, 1963.

*JSA-A* = *Journal of the Society of Archer-Antiquaries.*

Lepsius, *Denkmaeler* = C. R. Lepsius, *Denkmaeler aus Aegypten und Aethiopien, usw.*, 12 vols., Berlin 1849–59.

LUCAS–HARRIS = A. Lucas, *Ancient Egyptian Materials and Industries*, 4th edn., revised and enlarged by J. R. Harris, London, 1962.

PORTER–MOSS = B. Porter and R. L. B. Moss, *Topographical Bibliography of Ancient Egyptian Hieroglyphic Texts, Reliefs, and Paintings*, 7 vols., Oxford, 1927–51; 2nd edn., with the assistance of E. W. Burney, Oxford, 1960 and following.

*Toutankhamon* = C. Desroches-Noblecourt, *Vie et mort d'un pharaon: Toutankhamon*, Paris, 1963 (tr. *Tutankhamen: Life and Death of a Pharaoh*, London–New York, 1963).

*Treasure* = P. Fox, *Tutankhamun's Treasure*, London, 1951.

*Urk.* IV = *Urkunden des ägyptischen Altertums*, Abt. IV: *Urkunden der 18. Dynastie*, Heft 1–16 (ed. K. Sethe), Leipzig 1906–9, 1930; Heft 17–22 (ed. H. W. Helck), Berlin, 1955–8. *Übersetzung*, Heft 1–4 (K. Sethe), Leipzig, 1914; Heft 17–22 (H. W. Helck), Berlin, 1961.

*Wb.* = A. Erman and H. Grapow, *Wörterbuch der aegyptischen Sprache*, 7 vols., Leipzig–Berlin 1926–63, with *Belegstellen* to vols. I–V.

Wolf, *Bewaffnung* = W. Wolf, *Die Bewaffnung des altägyptischen Heeres*, Leipzig, 1926.

Wreszinski, *Atlas* = W. Wreszinski, *Atlas zur altaegyptischen Kulturgeschichte*, 3 vols., Leipzig, 1923–40.

See also below, pp. 4–5.

# INTRODUCTION

SOURCES OF INFORMATION

IN his preliminary report on the first season's work, Howard Carter describes how the finds from the tomb of Tutʿankhamūn were recorded. As the chamber was cleared, every object was assigned a catalogue number, and photographed *in situ* with its number attached. It was then transported to the 'workroom', in the tomb of Sethos II, where it was examined: 'measurements, complete archaeological notes, and copies of inscriptions were entered on the filing cards. The necessary mending and preservative treatment followed, after which it was taken just outside the entrance for scale photographs to be made' (CARTER–MACE, I, p. 163). Despite the frustrations and anxieties of the first seasons—the never-ending stream of visitors, Carnarvon's death, the impatience of the press, friction with the government, Mace's illness—Carter continued to display the same meticulous concern for detail throughout the decade he worked at the tomb. He intended eventually to present a final scientific publication, with a full description of its contents; but this project was cut short by his death on 2 March 1939. Subsequently his records of the work, including the index cards, were deposited in the Griffith Institute, Ashmolean Museum, Oxford.

When the contents of the tomb reached the Egyptian Museum in Cairo, they were registered under new inventory numbers in the *Journal d'Entrée du Musée*, together with brief descriptions. Each object also received an 'Exhibition number', which is written on labels in the display cases and is used in guide books. There is no list correlating Carter's Object numbers with the Museum's *Journal d'Entrée* numbers and Exhibition numbers.

Among the less publicized items from the treasure are the composite bows. Only ten other such instruments have survived from ancient Egypt, most of them fragmentary or damaged. Carter found at least twenty-nine in the tomb, all virtually complete and relatively well preserved. They are now in Cairo, seventeen on exhibition, the remainder in storage.

Carter's notes on the composite bows fill fifty-four index cards, $8 \times 5$ in.; these fall into two groups:

1. Forty-one cards describing the thirteen bows found in the Antechamber of the Tomb, the room from which the other chambers open; it was cleared in the first season, 1922/3. The written descriptions, with accompanying sketches (mostly to scale), were done by A. C. Mace. Following each description is a brief note by A. Lucas, 'on the preservative treatment employed' (CARTER–MACE, I, p. 164).

2. Thirteen cards describing the sixteen bows found in the Annexe or Store-room, the room heaped high with disorderly miscellanea, opening west off the Antechamber; clearing began here in the sixth season, 1927/8. The descriptions, which are less detailed and have fewer drawings than the earlier group, were done by Carter himself.

There are also ten photographs of the bows, taken by Harry Burton at Thebes during the course of the excavations. They provide considerable information about dimensions and decoration, and may be checked against the descriptions, as most of the bows photographed were labelled. Burton's negatives are at the Metropolitan Museum of Art, New York, with some duplicates at the Griffith Institute, Oxford.

## Decorative Motifs

Most of the bows are decorated in zones of fine geometric or naturalistic patterns, in coloured bark or inlay. Certain motifs are recurrent. In general, they are familiar from Egyptian art, both in funerary paintings (see especially P. Fořtová-Šámalová and M. Vilímková, *Egyptian Ornament*), and in other painted or inlaid objects from the tomb. In the catalogue, the motifs are designated by code-letters. Motifs *a–j* are found on the bark-covered bows; motifs *p–w* on the gold-covered 'Bow of Honour' (4).

(*a*) Lozenge chain [*c.* 0·002 broad];[1] a row of tangent diamonds, light on dark. Bows **1, 2, 5–9, 15, 16, 27, 28**; cf. child's chair (Obj. no. 39): Carter–Mace, I, pl. 59; staff (Obj. no. 50 *xx*): ibid., I, pl. 71*a*; stick (Obj. no. 100 *b*): ibid., I, pl. 71*b*; ceremonial baton (Obj. no. 227 *a*): ibid., II, pl. 8*b*; bow-case (Obj. no. 335): ibid., III, pls. 28*b*, 29*a, b*.

(*b₁*) Four-strand twist [*c.* 0·004/0·005 broad]; lattice-work, light on dark, composed of diagonal strips crossing each other at right angles; at the margin, the strips are joined, to form four overlapping zigzag lines. Bows **1, 7, 9, 15, 16, 28**; cf. staff (Obj. no. 50 *xx*): Carter–Mace, I, pl. 71*a*; ceremonial baton (Obj. no. 227 *a*): ibid., II, pl. 8*b*.

(*b₂*) Six-strand twist [*c.* 0·007 broad]; similar, but wider.  Bow **27**.

(*b*) Twist; similar, of uncertain width. Bows **6, 8**.

(*c*) Rhombic chequerboard [*c.* 0·006 broad]; three rows of lozenges, dark on light; the outer two rows have smaller light lozenges applied; the two borders are formed by rows of dark triangles. Bows **1, 9, 27, 28**; cf. ceremonial baton (Obj. no. 227 *a*): Carter–Mace, II, pl. 8*b*.

(*d*) Chequerboard [*c.* 0·006 broad]; four rows of rectangles, alternately dark and light. Bows **27, 28**; for this type of motif, see *Eg. Ornament*, nos. 2–10; cf. painted box (Obj. no. 21): Carter–Mace, I, pls. 50, 51, 52, 53, 54; ibid., II, pl. 3; stick (Obj. no. 100 *b*): ibid., I, pl. 71*b*; unguent vase (Obj. no. 579): ibid., III, pl. 48.

(*e*) Quadruple running chevron [*c.* 0·006 broad]; four zigzags, light in colour, separated by narrow dark lines; at the margin, a row of light triangles. Bows **1, 6, 9, 15, 27**; for this type of motif, see *Eg. Ornament*, nos. 18–21; cf. staff (Obj. no. 50 *xx*): Carter–Mace, I, pl. 71*a*.

(*f₁*) Simple petal garland [*c.* 0·006 broad]; on a dark ground, pendant from the distal margin, narrow light triangles, points towards the grip. Bows **1, 6, 7, 8**; for this type of motif, see *Eg. Ornament*, nos. 224–7; for examples of various types of petal garlands, see Obj. no. 40: Carter–Mace, I, pl. 56, and Obj. no. 577: ibid., III, pl. 44*b*; Obj. no. 39: ibid., I, pl. 59, and Obj. no. 351: ibid., III, pl. 33; Obj. no. 578: ibid., III, pls. 41, 74; Obj. no. 420: ibid., III, pl 49*a*; Obj. no. 211: ibid., II, pls. 50, 51, and Obj. no. 578: ibid., III, pl. 41; Obj. no. 579: ibid., III, pl. 48; Obj. no. 520: ibid., III, pl. 79*a*.

(*f₂*) The same reversed, with points towards tip. Bow **8**.

(*g₁*) Petal garland, festooned [*c.* 0·006 broad; *c.* 0·012 in **27, 28**]; light on dark, narrow triangles, pendant from the distal margin, points towards grip; the points of adjacent triangles are linked by light-coloured running chevrons; the upper angles of the chevrons touch the lower angles of the triangles, and the lower angles of the chevrons are tangent to the proximal margin; at about mid-height, the triangles are joined by a narrow light-coloured horizontal strip. Bows **1, 2, 6–9, 15,**

---

[1] For the signification of square brackets, see below, p. 4 (Dimensions and Descriptions).

**27, 28**; cf. staff (Obj. no. 50 *xx*): CARTER–MACE, I, pl. 71*a*; ceremonial baton (Obj. no. 227 *a*): ibid., II, pl. 8*b*; bow-case (Obj. no. 335): ibid., III, pl. 29*b*; fan stock (Obj. no. 600): ibid., III, pl. 43*c*.

($g_2$) The same reversed, with points towards tip. Bows **2, 5–9**.

($h_1$) Petal garland, festooned: two species [*c.* 0·006 broad]; as $g_1$, but with a smaller light triangle rising, point downward, from the lower angle of the chevron. Bow **9**.

($h_2$) The same reversed, with points towards tip. Bow **9**.

(*i*) Petal garland, festooned: two species, including lotus [*c.* 0·006 broad]; as $h_1$, but with a small dark square overlying the base of the large triangle. Bow **9**.

(*j*) Running spiral. Bow **2**; for this type of motif, see *Eg. Ornament*, nos. 143–6; cf. ceremonial baton (Obj. no. 227 *a*): CARTER–MACE, II, pl. 8*b*.

(*p*) Running spiral [*c.* 0·020 broad]: gold filigree pattern, with running spirals on a black ground, flanked on each side by three bands of simulated braid or rope, of which the central one is broadest. This is the border element of all decorated zones of Bow **4**.

(*q*) Superimposed chevrons [*c.* 0·004 broad], of varying colours; the usual sequence is dark blue, light blue, dark blue, fibrous calcite (?). Cf. *Eg. Ornament*, no. 50; also second state chariot (Obj. no. 122): CARTER–MACE, II, pls. 17*b*, 38; third coffin (Obj. no. 255): ibid., II, pls. 24, 71; second coffin (Obj. no. 254): ibid., II, pls. 68, 69; *Toutankhamon*, pl. 55; pectoral collars (Obj. nos. 256 *z*, 256 *mmm*, 256 *nnn*): CARTER–MACE, II, pls. 80*a, b*, 81*b*; 'ecclesiastical' throne (Obj. no. 351): ibid., III, pl. 33; *Toutankhamon*, pl. 12; miniature canopic coffins (Obj. no. 266 *g*): CARTER–MACE, III, pl. 54; *Toutankhamon*, pl. 34.

(*r*) Band of Circles [*c.* 0·004 broad]; gold inlaid with tiny circles of varying colours; the usual sequence is dark blue, light blue, dark blue, fibrous calcite (?). Cf. *Eg. Ornament*, nos. 124–5.

(*s*) Guilloche [*c.* 0·005 broad]; the sigmate elements are alternately dark blue and light blue glass; the ovals in the centre, and the triangles at the margin, are of gold. Cf. *Eg. Ornament*, no. 137 (a variety of running spiral); also axle of state chariot (Obj. no. 120 *a*): CARTER–MACE, II, pl. 39*b*, bottom.

(*t*) Lozenge chain [*c.* 0·003 broad]; gold lozenges; separated by marginal triangles of dark blue glass.

($u_1$) Stylized buds [*c.* 0·008 broad]; in the centre, a row of small circles, alternately dark blue and light blue glass; on the distal side of each circle is a triangle of gold, point towards tip; on the proximal side, a thin bar of gold. Between the gold bars are pentagons of fibrous calcite (?): between the gold triangles are circles of fibrous calcite (?).

($u_2$) Similar; the circles between the gold triangles are of light blue glass.

($v_1$) Palmettes and buds, alternating [*c.* 0·012 broad]; stalk of palmette, gold; seven leaves: dark blue, dark blue, light blue, dark blue, light blue, dark blue, dark blue; from centre of outer leaf, pendant gold curl. In centre of bud, circle of light blue [actually green; quite different from the light blue of the palmette]; stem and triangular top of bud, gold; on sides of triangular top, two tiny ovals of light blue [actually green].

($v_2$) Similar; the circle at the centre of the bud is white stone.

(*w*) Bead net [*c.* 0·025 broad]; the arms of the fretwork are dark blue glass; at the intersections of the arms are tiny round beads of gold. The lozenges and (at the edges) the triangles between the arms are of fibrous gypsum (?) [but it looks like what is called 'fibrous calcite (?)' above]. For this type of motif, see *Eg. Ornament*, nos. 91–2, 98–100; also ebony fan (Obj. no. 245): CARTER–MACE, II, pl. 63*a*; reed case (Obj. no. 271 *e* (1)): *Toutankhamon*, pl. 4*b*, top.

Motifs *a–j* are separated from each other, and from undecorated portions of the bow, by two or three thin light strips.

## EXPLANATION OF THE CATALOGUE

ANATOMY OF THE BOW. The 'grip' is that portion in the centre of the stave which is grasped when the bow is shot. The 'arm' (limb) is the main part of the stave, extending from the grip to the tip: 'lower arm' is that part of the arm near the grip; 'upper arm' is that part near the tip. The 'nock' is the notch or groove at the tip in which the bowstring is attached. The 'back' is the side of the bow away from the archer when he shoots; in a reflexed bow, such as those in the present catalogue, the back is the concave side when the bow is unstrung. The 'face' or 'belly' is the side towards the archer when he shoots.

THE ORDER OF THE CATALOGUE follows the order of the Object numbers.

DIMENSIONS. All measurements are in metres. Lengths transcribed from the *Journal d'Entrée* are so labelled; other unbracketed measurements are either specified in Mace's or Carter's notes, or measured from a scaled section. Measurements enclosed within square brackets must be regarded as approximations; most of them are estimated from sketches or photographs, a few are calculated from other data in the notes. When the dimensions of a cross-section are given, the width (side to side) precedes the thickness (back to face).

DESCRIPTIONS are based primarily on the notes of Mace and Carter, though these have been edited, emended, and rearranged.[1] Further details have been added from Burton's photographs without comment. Descriptive data enclosed within square brackets have been added by B. Turzynski, from personal observation of the bows in Cairo. The decoration of each bow is described in zones, beginning at the grip and working towards the tips; each zone of decoration is likewise described from grip towards the tips.

INSCRIPTIONS. The translations of the hieroglyphic inscriptions, and some notes on the texts, have been contributed by D. B. Redford. Fourteen of the bows bear inscriptions on panels on the face of the stave. These always differ in the two limbs.

ABBREVIATIONS

| | |
|---|---|
| B.T. | B. Turzynski |
| CM | Cairo, Egyptian Museum |
| Ed. | Editor |
| est. | estimated |

---

[1] It may seem presumptuous in the circumstances to alter details of description given in the field-notes. To exonerate myself I offer a few examples. Mace locates the rectangular inscribed panels on the 'outside' or 'outer side' (**1, 2, 3, 5, 6, 7, 8, 9, 10, 11, 12**); read 'face' (Plate IV). Carter puts the panels, inscribed or decorated, on the 'back' (**15, 16, 19, 21, 22, 24**); read 'face' (Plates IX, XII). Mace locates the vertical groove at the nock on the 'back' (**5, 7,** 9); read 'face'. He describes the hieroglyphs as 'headed outwards' or 'heading towards the end, or tip' (**5, 6, 7, 8, 9, 10**); he means 'with the heads towards the tip, but reading from the tip towards the grip' (Plate IV). Carter calls the concave side the 'belly' (**14, 15, 16, 17, 19, 20, 22, 23**); read 'back'. He also ascribes the double-curved profile to 'warping' (**14, 15, 16, 17, 19, 29**). He designates two of the bows as 'self-bows' (**19, 20**).

Exhib. no.    Exhibition number; Guide number; number in *Description sommaire des principaux monuments/ A Brief Description of the Principal Monuments*

GI    Griffith Institute, Oxford

G.T.M.    G. T. Martin

J.E.    *Journal d'Entrée du Musée du Caire*

L. (pr.)    Length (preserved)

MMA    Metropolitan Museum of Art, New York

neg.    negative (photographic)

Obj. no.    Object number assigned by Carter (called 'catalogue number', CARTER–MACE, I, p. 128; 'registration number', ibid., I, p. 163).

See also above, p. viii.

# CATALOGUE

## Composite Bows described in Carter's Notes

**1.** Double composite angular bow. Obj. no. 48 *f*; J.E. 61545; Exhib. no. 520 (identification by CM, in J.E. and PORTER–MOSS, I. ii², p. 581). Mentioned: McLeod, *AJA*, 66 (1962), p. 18, n. 38. Photographs: whole bow, from side, Plate III; grip and lower arm, from face, Plate IV; tip, from side, Plate V. Description by Mace (two cards). 'Treated with melted paraffin wax' (Lucas). On display, CM, Room 30, case 75, no. 5.

The Object number 48 is assigned to a group of staves and bows laid casually on a bed of ebony and woven cord (Obj. no. 47) which stood on a lion-headed couch (Obj. no. 35) at the north end of the west wall of the Antechamber; this group of objects is mentioned, CARTER–MACE, I, p. 113; *Treasure*, p. 18; pictures *in situ*, CARTER–MACE, I, pls. 16, 17. Photographs: *in situ*, Plate I; on bed, Plate II. Discovered in the first season (1922/3).

When found, this bow was entirely enveloped in a strip of linen about 0·11 wide, which was wrapped around it.

L., 1·12 (Mace); 1·10 (J.E.). Grip oval in section. [*c.* 0·02 × 0·015]. The grip [for 0·23] is single; but from this point out to the tips, each arm is double, terminating in two independent nocks, side by side. Structure concealed by bark covering.

(i) Grip [0·08], plain light [yellowish-brown] bark.

(ii) Lower arm [0·07/0·08], decorated zone with motifs (in one arm) $a$ - $c$ - $e$ - $a$ - $g_1$ - $a$ - $e$ - $a$ - $c$ - $a$; (in other arm) the same, but with the first motif repeated ($a$ - $a$ - $c$ - $e$ - etc.). Colours: light on dark [gold, black, dark red].

(iii) Most of each pair of arms [0·31/0·32], plain light [yellowish-brown] bark; on the face of each pair of arms, a dark rectangular panel, 0·145 long [beginning about 0·045 from the end of zone (ii)]. In each panel, a hieroglyphic inscription in light bark, reading from tip towards grip; each pair of arms bears the same text, but in mirror-image, facing the mid line.

Inscription 1. 1 (Plate XVI)

> 'The good god, son of Amūn, whom the king of the gods created, king of Upper and Lower Egypt, lord of the Two Lands, master of the cultus, Nebkheprurēʿ, given life eternally (or, may he be given life eternally).'

Inscription 1. 2 (Plate IV; Plate XVI)

> 'The good god, strong of bow,[1] possessed of might, vigorous in drawing it, son of Rēʿ, lord of diadems, Tutʿankhaten, like Rēʿ.'[2]

---

[1] Singular (?), the plural strokes perhaps derived from ⌂|||𓀀, 'battalion'. The phrase *nḫt pḏt* recurs in Inscriptions 5. 1, 10. 2, 13. 2, 15. 1, 19. 1; and cf. *Urk.* IV. 2058. 23, 2059. 4. See also note on Inscription 2. 4 below.

[2] Has some verb been omitted before *mi rʿ*? The usual construction finds some such verb as *ʿnḫ*, *wȝḥ*, or *di ʿnḫ* before *mi rʿ*; e.g. *Wb.* II. 37. 5, and Inscriptions 4. 4, 10. 2, 11. 1. The phrase *mi rʿ* without preceding verb recurs in Inscriptions 6. 2, 8. 1, 9. 2, 12. 2; and cf. *Urk.* IV. 2059. 20. See also note on Inscription 19. 2 below.

(iv) Upper arm [0·10], decorated zone with motifs (in one of each pair of arms) $a$ - $b_1$ - $a$ - $e$ - $b_1$ - $a$ - $g_1$ - $a$ - $f_1$ - $a$ - $b_1$ - $a$ - $e$ - $a$ - $g_1$ - $b_1$ - $a$; (in the other arm of each pair) the same, but with an additional lozenge chain in fifth place ($a$ - $b_1$ - $a$ - $e$ - $a$ - $b_1$ - etc.). Colours: light on dark. This zone bounded on the side closest the tips by six thin light strips running around the staves.

(v) Tip [0·06/0·05], plain dark bark; the knob beyond the nock is covered with plain light bark.[1] Nock: Plate xv.

The double-tipped bow is a rarity. A fragment in New York (*AJA*, 66 [1962], pp. 17–18, no. 4) may be from a similar weapon; its core at the grip is made up of two staves. One's first instinct would be to recognize them as 'pellet bows', with a pair of strings supporting a pocket for the bullet. But such weapons usually have provision for the stone to pass forward without striking the centre of the bow or the bow hand: sometimes the grip is offset—but this is not so in the Egyptian bows. More commonly the bowstave is turned sideways before shooting—a practice which would not be possible with double tips. The objections to this interpretation seem decisive. Modern composite bows (from India and elsewhere) with double tips are apparently so designed to compensate for the poor lateral stability of the bows, and to prevent the staves from twisting. But in them it is only the extremity of the limb which is doubled.[2] The purpose of the long double limbs of the Tutꜥankhamūn bow remains obscure.

**2.** Composite angular bow. Obj. no. 48 *g* (1); J.E. 61524; Exhib. no. 523 (identification confirmed by B.T. on the basis of the inscriptions). Description by Mace (three cards). 'Sprayed with celluloid in amyl acetate; treated with melted paraffin wax' (Lucas). On display, CM, Room 30, case 109, third from top.

Provenience, as for **1**. This bow was found with **3**, the two being bound together by a strip of linen about 0·07 wide, which was wrapped round and round, and tied loosely at the ends.

L., 1·315 (Mace's notes and sketch); 1·125 (J.E.; probably an error for 1·315, which is wrongly ascribed to the preceding entry in J.E., the two lengths being interchanged). Grip almost round in section, 0·024 × 0·023; upper arm, 0·017 × 0·013. Structure almost totally concealed by bark covering. In a tentative sketch Mace indicated that he could distinguish facing and backing strips as well as one side strip applied to the core; he did not indicate the material.

[1] Mace thus describes one pair of arms; for the other he says 'plain light bark'. B.T. states that both pairs of tips are the same.

[2] On the pellet bow, see G. Antze, 'Einige Bemerkungen zu den Kugelbogen im städtischen Museums für Völkerkunde zu Leipzig', *Jahrbuch des städt. Mus. f. Völkerk. zu Leipzig*, 3 (1908/9), pp. 79–95; C. Grayson, 'Stone Bows', *JSA-A*, 9 (1966), pp. 32–4. On the stone bow of the arbalest type see Sir R. Payne-Gallwey, *The Crossbow, Mediaeval and Modern, Military and Sporting: Its Construction, History, and Management, with a Treatise on the Balista and Catapult of the Ancients and an Appendix on the Catapult, Balista, and the Turkish Bow* (London, 1903/7: repr. London, 1958), pp. 157–62, 177–200. Almost invariably stone bows (of either type) are not double, but have a single nock at each tip. Oriental composite bows with double tips include Istanbul, Topkapı Saray, Salle d'Armes, no. 8857 (Turkish; the part of the arm which is double is 0·12 at each end); British Museum, Acc. no. 96–1197 ('Indo-Persian', from the collection of the antiquary Charles Franks; ears double for 0·09); Victoria and Albert Museum, Acc. no. 3487 (from Ahmadnagar, about 50 miles north-east of Ahmadabad; string intact; ears double for 0·075); Smithsonian Institution, Cat. no. 272,897 (from Persia; ears double for 0·07 at one tip, 0·085 at the other; described by H. S. Hamlin, 'The Persian Bow', *Archery*, NFAA, May, 1948); Smithsonian Institution, Cat. no. 349,825 (Tatar, from North China; ears double for 0·054). The explanation was suggested by Lt.-Cdr. W. F. Paterson, *Newsletter of the Society of Archer-Antiquaries*, 15 (July 1967), p. 2, no. 14. I am pleased to acknowledge the guidance of Lt.-Cdr. Paterson in compiling this note. I am also grateful to R. H. Pinder-Wilson of the Department of Oriental Antiquities of the British Museum, to John Lowry of the Indian Section of the Victoria and Albert Museum, and to Robert A. Elder of the Office of Anthropology of the United States National Museum (Smithsonian Institution) for sending details of the bows mentioned above.

(i) Grip and lower arms [0·540], plain medium bark [light brown as in **6** and **8**]; on the face of each arm, a rectangular panel of dark bark, 0·115 long [beginning about 0·12 from the centre of the grip and] extending to 0·035 from the end of this zone. In each panel, a hieroglyphic inscription in medium bark, reading from tip towards grip, with a *sma* symbol below.

Inscription 2. 1 (Plate XVI)

'*The good god, strong of arm, lord of the Two Lands, Nebkheprurēʿ.*'

Inscription 2. 2 (Plate XVI)

'*Son of Rēʿ, of his body, his beloved, lord of diadems, crusher of the Nine Bows, Tutʿankhamūn— ruler-of-Southern-Heliopolis.*'

(ii) Mid arm [0·04/0·03], decorated inscribed zone; [motifs $g_1$ - $a$]; colours: very light on medium bark [red, gold, light on black]. In the centre, dark band, 0·02 wide, bearing circumferent hieroglyphic inscription in medium bark; the top of the inscription is toward the tips. [Then motifs $a$ - $g_2$.]

Inscription 2. 3 (Plate XVI)

'*The good god, lord of the Two Lands, master of the cultus, strong of arm, Nebkheprurēʿ.*'

Inscription 2. 4 (Plate XVI)

'*The good god, vigorous with the bow* (or, *the valiant, strong of bow*)[1], *lord of the Two Lands, Nebkheprurēʿ.*'

(iii) Upper arm [0·290], plain medium bark.

(iv) Near tip [0·025], decorated zone [with motifs $a$ - $j$ - $a$]; colours: light on medium bark [gold and light on black].

(v) Tip [0·05/0·06], plain dark bark; the knob beyond the nock is covered with medium [i.e. light] bark. Nock: Plate XV.

**3.** Composite angular bow. Obj. no. 48 *g* (2); J.E. 61520; Exhib. no. 3113 (identification by CM, PORTER–MOSS, I. ii², p. 581) Description by Mace (two cards). 'Sprayed with celluloid in amyl acetate; treated with melted paraffin wax' (Lucas). In storage, CM, Tut. Magazine, box M.

Provenience, as for **2.**

L., 1·26 (Mace; J.E.). Section elliptical, with face flattened; grip, 0·025×0·018; upper arm, 0·015×0·009; collar below nock, 0·015×0·016. Structure concealed by bark covering.

(i) Grip and lower arms [0·57], plain light bark; on the face of each arm, a rectangular dark panel, 0·18 long [beginning about 0·14 from the centre of the grip and] extending to 0·01 from the end of this zone. In each panel, a hieroglyphic inscription in light bark, reading from tip towards grip, and framed by symbols for myriads of years.

---

[1] The reading ⌂, confirmed by G.T.M., may represent either *ḳn pḏt* (assuming dittography) or *ḳn nḫt pḏt*, with *ḳn* an independent epithet. The latter interpretation is perhaps the more likely in that the phrase *nḫt pḏt* occurs in Inscriptions 1. 2, 5. 1, 10. 2, 13. 2, 15. 1, 19. 1, and a similar combination, *ḳn nḫt ḫpš* in Inscription 6. 1. [Ed.]

Inscription 3. 1 (Plate xvi)

> '*The good god, appearing in the white crown, lord of the sunlight which brightens* (?) *the face* (literally *lord of rays in the face*),[1] *like Aten, king of Upper and Lower Egypt, lord of the Two Lands, master of the cultus, strong of arm, Nebkheprurēʿ.*'

Inscription 3. 2 (Plate xvi)

> '*The good god, loud of battle-cry, possessed of power, like the son of Nut,*[2] *son of Rēʿ, of his body, his beloved, lord of diadems, Tutʿankhamūn—ruler-of-Southern-Heliopolis.*'

(ii) Mid arm [0·03], decorated inscribed zone; band of dark bark, outlined on each side by five lines of light bark. Cartouches in light bark, on face, *Nebkheprurēʿ*, on back, *Tutʿankhamūn*, flanked by uraei; details of uraei in inlay or paint.

(iii) Upper arm [0·21/0·22], plain light bark.

(iv) Near tip [0·07], decorated inscribed zone; patterns of light bark on dark (details of motifs not available); in the centre, a circumferent band, 0·012 wide, bearing the cartouches, *Nebkheprurēʿ Tutʿankhamūn*.

(v) Tip [0·06], plain dark bark; the knob beyond the nock is covered with light bark. Nock: Plate xv.

**4.** Composite angular 'Bow of Honour', covered with sheet gold. Obj. no. 48 *h*; J.E. 61517; Exhib. no. 120 (identification by CM, J.E.). Mentioned: CARTER–MACE, I, p. 113; II, p. 15; *Treasure*, p. 18. Photographs: whole bow, from side, Plate III; grip and lower arm from face, Plate IV; from back, Plate VI; tip, from side, Plates V, VII. Description by Mace (seven cards). 'Cleaned with damp brush; sprayed with celluloid in amyl acetate' (Lucas). On display, CM, Room 30, case 75, no. 4.

Provenience, as for **1**. When found, this bow was covered with a linen bandage about 0·09 wide; its end was carried down the bow about 0·20, and then wrapped round and round, and tied at the other end in a granny knot.

L., 1·34 (Mace); 1·33 (emended from J.E., which gives 0·133). Section at grip almost round, 0·027 × 0·025; in mid arm, elliptical, 0·032 × 0·02; upper arm, 0·017 × 0·011; collar below nock, 0·02 × 0·03. Details of construction are concealed by gold sheeting and fine filigree gold-work inlaid with coloured stones and glass. The bow is not completely covered with gold sheeting in a single piece; rather, each plain band is composed of a single piece of gold; the decorative bands overlap it at each edge for a width of 0·004.

(i) Centre of grip [0·03], plain sheet gold.

(ii) Outer edge of grip [0·03], inscribed zone; band of a black gummy substance, on which gold pattern and hieroglyphs were stuck. At each edge of the band, a guilloche border; in the centre, a circumferent hieroglyphic inscription, its top toward the tips.

---

[1] For the expression, cf. B.M. stela no. 826 (Suty and Hor), line 2 (I. E. S. Edwards, *Hieroglyphic Texts from Egyptian Stelae, etc., in the British Museum*, VIII [London, 1939], pl. 21): *stwt.k m ḥr n rḫ.tw.s*, 'thy rays fall on the face (even) when one is not aware of it'; Theban tomb no. 65 (Imiseba) ⟨652⟩ (*Wb. Belegstellen*, IV. 331. 10): *mȝn.k itn tp dwȝyt ʿbʿb stwt.f n ḥr.k*, 'mayest thou see the sun disc at morning, may its rays be resplendent in thy face'. The word *stwt*, of course, occupies an important place in the Amarna sun-hymns; e.g. the great Aten hymn: N. de G. Davies, *The Rock Tombs of El Amarna*, 6 [London, 1908], pl. 32.

[2] The correct reading 𓊨𓇋𓅆𓏏 confirmed by G.T.M.; for the expression 'son of Nut' applied to Tutʿankhamūn, cf. *Urk.* IV. 2049. 20, 2055. 4, 2059. 18.

Inscription 4. 1 (Plate XVII)

'*King of Upper and Lower Egypt, lord of the Two Lands, possessed of might, Nebkheprurēʿ.*'[1]

Inscription 4. 2 (Plate XVII)

'*Son of Rēʿ, of his body, his beloved,*[2] *Nebkheprurēʿ.*'[1]

(iii) Adjoining grip [0·03], plain sheet gold.

(iv) Lower arm [0·08], decorated zone with motifs $p - q - s - q - v_2 - q - s - p$.

(v) Lower arm [0·03], plain sheet gold.

(vi) Lower arm [0·075], decorated zone with motifs $p - s - w - s - p$.

(vii) Mid arm [0·03], plain sheet gold.

(viii) Mid arm [0·08], decorated zone with motifs $p - q - s - q - v_1 - q - s - q - p$.

(ix) Mid arm [0·03], plain sheet gold.

(x) Upper arm [0·075], decorated zone with motifs $p - r - s - r - v_1 - r - s - p$.

(xi) Upper arm [0·03], plain sheet gold.

(xii) Upper arm [0·11/0·12], decorated zone with motifs $p - s - t - u_2 - u_2 - t - s - p - s - q - t - u_1 - t - q - s - p$ [in one arm; in the other arm the third last motif is omitted, so that the sequence closes $- u_1 - t - s - p$]. (In the latter arm the innermost edge of this zone had broken and come loose in antiquity; it had been bound round with a thin slip of papyrus.)

(xiii) Near tip [0·02], plain sheet gold.

---

[1] The inept disposition of the signs within the cartouches of Inscriptions 4. 1, 4. 2, clearly visible in the photograph (Plate IV, enlargements Plate XXa, b), suggested that these might not be original. The details were therefore carefully checked by G.T.M., who, while not able to handle the bow, examined it through the glass of the case by daylight and with the aid of a torch. That both cartouches had in fact been modified was amply confirmed, though the method employed was not the same. In the case of Inscription 4. 2, the former cartouche (on a black ground, with hieroglyphs in gold leaf) was overlaid with a strip of brown material bearing the new prenomen (in reverse!); traces of what are presumably the original signs protrude above the upper edge of the strip (Plate XXd). In the case of Inscription 4. 1, the minimum alteration was made to the hieroglyphs on the existing black ground, the result being rather clumsy. Three of the signs (⊙, 𓋹, ɪɪɪ) appear to be part of the original cartouche; the fourth (▽) has been added, and is badly positioned, touching the border of the cartouche. Traces of some of the hieroglyphs effaced by the usurpation survive as follows (Plate XXc):

(i) below ⊙: faint traces of a sign rounded at the top and with two strokes meeting at right angles beneath (almost certainly 𓊽);

(ii) above ɪɪɪ: clear traces of an oblong sign (▭, for ▭);

(iii) above ▽: very faint traces—on the right a circular sign (probably ⊙), on the left something indistinct, with a particle of gold leaf;

(iv) below ▽: further faint traces—on the right a rough speck, on the left apparently plural strokes (ɪɪɪ).

On the basis of what remains, the most plausible reconstruction of the original cartouche is ʿnḫ-ḫprw-rʿ mry nfr-ḫprw-rʿ (Plate XXe), i.e. one of the several variants of the prenomen of Smenkhkarēʿ. The same form, with minor differences in the writing, occurs on parts of two similar boxes (Obj. nos. 1 k, 574: Plate XXf, g), on a pair of faience bracelets (Obj. nos. 620 (41, 42): Plate XXh), on trappings from the mummy (Obj. nos. 256 a, b (4)), on rings from El-Amarna (Plate XXi), and perhaps also in a graffito in Theban tomb 139 (Pairy) (cf. *JEA*, 14 [1928], pl. 5), the compressed arrangement of the signs in the present instance having presumably been dictated by considerations of space. On the boxes and in the graffito the accompanying nomen is of the form nfr-nfrw-itn mry wʿ-n-rʿ, while on the bracelets it would appear to be nfr-nfrw-itn mry iḥ-n-itn (elsewhere combined with the prenomen ʿnḫ-ḫprw-rʿ mry wʿ-n-rʿ). If either was what stood originally within the cartouche of Inscription 4. 2, the signs will likewise have been rather cramped. The replacement of the cartouches within the existing borders may account for the fact that in both instances, and again in Inscriptions 4. 3, 4. 4, the new prenomen alone is repeated, whereas on every other bow Nebkheprurēʿ is balanced by Tutʿankhamūn in corresponding inscriptions. [Ed.]

[2] The ◠ presumably by attraction from ḫt.f; cf. Inscription 6. 2.

(xiv) Near tip [0·01], inscribed zone; band of a black gummy substance; applied to it, a narrow gold border, and a circumferent hieroglyphic inscription, its top towards the tip.

Inscription 4. 3 (Plate XVII)

'*The good ruler*,[1] *the valiant*,[2] *lord of the Two Lands, Nebkheprurēʿ*.'

Inscription 4. 4 (Plate XVII)

'*Nebkheprurēʿ, given life like Rēʿ* (or, *may he be given life like Rēʿ*).'

(xv) Tip [0·04], plain sheet gold. Nock: Plate XV.

Bows decorated with gold are not unexampled. The Brooklyn bow (*AJA*, 62 [1958], p. 400) may have been covered with a gold wash. In the specimens from the tomb sheet gold is sometimes employed; thus, **14**, with bands on the arms; **29**, with one gilt tip; and of the self bows, six have the grip and tips covered with gold; and two more are completely encased with gold, and evidently intended never to be used. Because the gold of the 'Bow of Honour' is not continuous, but is applied in zones, presumably it could have been strung.

In this connection it is worth remembering that among the gifts sent by Tushratta to Amenophis III was at least one bow, no doubt composite, covered with gold.[3]

**5.** Double composite angular 'captive' bow. Obj. no. 48 *i* (1); J.E. 61544; Exhib. no. 127 (identification by CM, J.E., and PORTER–MOSS, I. ii², p. 581). Mentioned: CARTER–MACE, I, p. 113; *Treasure*, p. 18; McLeod, *AJA*, 66 (1962), p. 18, n. 38. Photographs: whole bow, from side, Plate III; grip and lower arm, from face, Plate IV; tip, from side, Plate V. Description by Mace (six cards). 'Sprayed with celluloid in amyl acetate; treated with melted paraffin wax' (Lucas). On display, CM, Room 30, case 75, no. 2.

Provenience, as for **1**. This bow was found with **6**, the two being bound together with a strip of linen 0·135 wide, which was wrapped round and round, and lightly tied with a single knot at one end.

L., 1·395 (Mace); 1·39 (J.E.). Grip and most of arms made up of two bows glued side by side; at the tips, for the terminal 0·07, the two staves are bound together and decorated as a single bow-stave. Section, at grip, 0·025 × 0·017; at mid arm, 0·025 × 0·015; upper arm, 0·012 × 0·008; collar below nock (shoulders of captive), 0·015 × 015. Structure concealed by bark covering.

(i) Grip [0·09], plain light [yellowish-brown] bark.

(ii) Beside grip [0.03], inscribed zone; black band with lozenge-chain borders and cartouches applied in light bark. Each bow has three cartouches in each arm, top towards tip, *Nebkheprurēʿ* on the back and face, and *Tutʿankhamūn* on the side.

(iii) Most of arm [0·55]; one bow covered with black bark, the other with light yellow bark. On the face of each bow of each arm is a rectangular panel, 0·076 long, beginning 0·09 from zone (ii),

---

[1] The reading ⌐⌐ (where *nṯr nfr* might be expected) is confirmed by the photograph (Plate V). [Ed.]

[2] The writing ◿ is as copied on Mace's card; it has not been possible to check this. [Ed.]

[3] J. A. Knudtzon, *Die El-Amarna-Tafeln*, I (Leipzig, 1915), p. 159, no. 22, col. i, lines 42–3: '*6 sekel of gold were used*'; 'no doubt composite', Bonnet, *Waffen*, p. 137, n. 2. Possibly another bow of different type, perhaps called

'angular', covered with 4 sekel of gold: Knudtzon, loc. cit., lines 36–7; see H. W. Helck, *Die Beziehungen Ägyptens zu Vorderasien im 3. and 2. Jahrtausend v. Chr.* (Wiesbaden, 1962), p. 444. Possibly also, according to Helck's interpretation, Tushratta sent 100 more 'angular' bows, with gold [coverings]: Knudtzon, op. cit., p. 173: no. 22, col. iii, lines 45–6.

I cannot forbear to cite Artemis' bow of solid gold, *Homeric Hymn*, 27. 5; cf. *Aeneid*, xi. 652, **774.**

containing a hieroglyphic inscription: on the black bow, a light panel and green [now very dark, almost black] hieroglyphs; on the yellow bow, a black panel with light hieroglyphs. The inscriptions read from tip towards grip.

Inscription 5. 1 (Plate IV; Plate XVII)

'*The good god, strong of bow, possessed of might, who fights hundreds of thousands, lord of the Two Lands, Nebkheprurēʿ, slaying the foreign lands.*'[1]

Inscription 5. 2 (Plate IV; Plate XVII)

'*Son of Rēʿ, of his body, his beloved, lord of diadems, lord of every foreign land, Tutʿankhamūn—ruler-of-Southern-Heliopolis, strong of arm.*'

Inscription 5. 3 (Plate XVII)

'*The good god, the valiant, mighty[2] over the foreign lands, lord of the Two Lands,[3] Nebkheprurēʿ, slaying the foreign lands.*'

Inscription 5. 4 (Plate XVII)

'*Son of Rēʿ, of his body, his beloved, who makes his own boundary,[4] lord of diadems, Tutʿankhamūn—ruler-of-Southern-Heliopolis, crusher of foreign lands.*'

(iv) Upper arm [0·02], decorated zone with motifs $a$ - $g_2$ - $a$ - $a$.

(v) Tip [0·065], the figure of a bound captive, facing the back of the bow; his head forms the knob beyond the nock, his neck is the nock, his shoulders form the collar below the nock; the drawn-together shoulder-blades form the groove for the string on the face of the bow (Plate XV).

At one tip, an African captive, with his arms bound behind his back at the shoulders. Face, chest, and arms, of black bark; hair or cap of red bark; details of eye, light yellow bark. Collar, tiny strips of gold; arm bindings, five bands of very light bark and four bands of red bark, alternating; bangle, gold leaf; diagonal brace, gold with a red bar. Skirt multicoloured, two shades of light bark, red bark, and gold leaf.

At the other tip, an Asiatic prisoner, with his arms bound behind his back at the elbows. Face, neck, and arms, of reddish bark; hair, beard, pupils of eyes, black bark; fillet around head, and details of face, in light bark. Elaborate variegated robe, light bark, lighter yellow bark, red bark, green bark, black bark; a few border details picked out in thin strips of gold leaf.

This bow embodied the conceit that every time the king drew it he garrotted two enemy captives. Plastic bowtips are not unusual elsewhere; it will suffice to refer to the birds' heads at the extremities of Assyrian, neo-Hittite, and Iranian bows.[5] And Asiatic and African captives are regular motifs on

---

[1] For the actual form of the sign ᗰᗯ, here and elsewhere, cf. the photograph (Plate IV). [Ed.]

[2] The reading 𓏺 established by G.T.M.; for the phrase *ṯnr ḥr ḫꜣswt*, cf. *Wb.* v. 383. 8. [Ed.]

[3] Reading *nb tꜣwy*.

[4] The traces, as verified by G.T.M., suggest the reading *ir n.f tꜣš.f*, with *ir* the perfective active participle (cf. A. H. Gardiner, *Egyptian Grammar*, 3rd edn., § 359, no. 36) and *n.f* reflexive; literally '*who makes his boundary for himself*'. [Ed.]

[5] On Assyrian plastic bow tips—not merely ducks'

heads, but also birds of prey, and even lions—see most recently B. Hrouda, *Die Kulturgeschichte des assyrischen Flachbildes* (*Saarbrücker Beiträge zur Altertumskunde* 2, Bonn, 1965), p. 83; cf. also W. Houghton, 'The Birds of the Assyrian Monuments and Records', *Trans. Soc. Bibl. Arch.*, 8 (1885), pp. 42–142, esp. 57, 133, and pl. 10, opp. p. 108. The bow in a relief from Zincirli has ducks' heads at the tips (F. von Luschan, in *Festschrift für Otto Benndorf* [Vienna, 1898], pl. 10). Bows terminating in ducks' heads are presented as tribute to Xerxes by the Susian delegation objects from the tomb of Tutᶜankhamūn (e.g. walking-sticks, Obj. nos. 48 *b*, 48 *c*, 50 *uu*, CARTER–MACE, I, pls. 69, 70; *Treasure*, pl. 14; yoke of state chariot, Obj. no. 120 *d*, CARTER–MACE, II, pl. 41). But this is the only extant Egyptian bow with modelled tips; it thus fills the gap noted by Bonnet, *Waffen*, pp. 143–4.

**6.** Composite angular bow. Obj. no. 48 *i* (2); J.E. 61537; Exhib. no. 119 (identification confirmed by B.T. on the basis of the inscriptions). Description by Mace (two cards). 'Sprayed with celluloid in amyl acetate; treated with melted paraffin wax' (Lucas). On display, CM, Room 30, case 109, second from top.

Provenience, as for **5**.

L., 1·20 (Mace); 1·19 (J.E.). Section oval; grip, 0·02 × 0·018; mid arm, 0·02 × 0·015; upper arm, 0·012 × 0·008; collar below nock, 0·014 × 0·014. Structure concealed by bark covering.

(i) Grip [0·14], plain dark yellow bark [actually light brown, as in **8**].

(ii) Lower arm [0·08], decorated zone [with motifs $a$ - $a$ - $b$ - $g_2$ - $e$; then a wider band decorated with a lozenge chequerboard, six rows of gold diamonds on black; then motifs $e$ - $g_1$ - $b$ - $a$ - $a$]. Colours: dark red ground, patterns in green [now very dark, almost black], and two shades of yellow.

(iii) Most of arm [0·33/0·36], plain dark yellow bark [actually light brown]; on the face, a black rectangular panel, 0·13 long, beginning 0·037 from the end of zone (ii). In the panel, a hieroglyphic inscription in dark yellow, reading from tip to grip.

Inscription 6. 1 (Plate XVII)

'*The good god, the valiant, strong of arm, king of Upper and Lower Egypt, lord of the Two Lands, Nebkheprurēᶜ, given life* (or, *may he be given life*).'

Inscription 6. 2 (Plate XVII)

'*Son of Rēᶜ, of his body, his beloved,*[1] *lord of diadems, the subduer of the Nine Bows, Tutᶜankhaten, like Rēᶜ eternally.*'

(iv) Upper arm [0·075], decorated zone [with motifs $a$ - $a$ - $b$ - $g_1$ - $a$ - $f_1$ - $b$; then a wider band decorated with a lozenge chequerboard; on a black ground, rows of gold diamonds; on the intervening reserved black diamonds, small gold diamonds or dots; then motifs $b$ - $f_1$ - $a$ - $g_1$ - $b$ - $a$]. Colours, as in zone (ii).

(v) Tip [0·05/0·04], plain black bark; the knob beyond the nock is covered with dark yellow.

**7.** Composite angular bow. Obj. no 48 *j* (1); J.E. 61525; Exhib. no. 128 (identification by CM, J.E.; confirmed by B.T. on the basis of the inscriptions). Photographs: whole bow, from side, Plate III; grip and lower arm, from back, Plate VI; tip, from side, Plate VII. Description by Mace (three cards).

in a relief from the Apadana at Persepolis (E. F. Schmidt, *Persepolis*, I [Chicago, 1953], pl. 28).

S. Dow refers me to the Apollo of Cyrene in the British Museum; he bears as one of his attributes a bow in the round, terminating in a griffin's head (see A. H. Smith, *Catalogue of Sculpture in the Department of Greek and* *Roman Antiquities, British Museum*, II [London, 1900], p. 223, no. 1380); probably a copy of an original of the second century B.C. by Timarchides I of Athens (see G. Becatti, *BullComm*, 63 [1935/6], pp. 111–31).

[1] See note on Inscription 4. 2 above.

'Sprayed with celluloid in amyl acetate; treated with melted paraffin wax' (Lucas). On display, CM, Room 30, case 75, no. 6.

Provenience, as for **1**. This bow was found with **8**, wrapped in a linen bandage about 0·07 wide; one end of the cloth was doubled down the bows for about 0·05, wound about them both for the complete length, and then tied in a loose knot at the other end.

L., 1·105 (Mace); 1·12 (emended from J.E., which gives 0·112). Section elliptical; grip, 0·02 × 0·015; mid arm, 0·02 × 0·012; upper arm, 0·011 × 0·008; collar below nock, 0·012 × 0·012. Structure largely concealed by bark covering; Mace does indicate that the core was surrounded on at least three sides by thin strips—the two sides and either the face or the back; he does not specify the material.

(i) Grip [0·12], alternating bands of plain light brown and of black, five of the former, four of the latter, each 0·013 wide.

(ii) Lower arm [0·07/0·08], decorated zone with motifs $a$ - $a$ - $b_1$ - $g_2$ - $a$; colours, light brown bark and gold leaf. In the centre, a band 0·02 wide, of dark red bark, with disc and branch pattern (?) [running lozenges in two parallel rows, making a figure-eight around the discs], in dark yellow. Then, motifs $a$ - $g_1$ - $b_1$ - $a$ - $a$.

(iii) Most of arm [0·27/0·25], plain light brown bark. On the face, a rectangular black panel, 0·145 long, beginning 0·044 above zone (ii). In the panel, a hieroglyphic inscription in light brown bark, reading from tip to grip.

Inscription 7. 1 (Plate XVII)

'*The good god, who acts with his (own) two arms, who subdues the Nine Bows through the terror he inspires* (literally, *through terror of him*), *king of Upper and Lower Egypt, lord of the Two Lands, master of the cultus, Nebkheprurēꜥ.*'

Inscription 7. 2 (Plate XVII)

'*Son of Rēꜥ, of his body, his beloved,*[1] *lord of diadems, beloved of Amūn, possessed of might, who fights against hundreds of thousands, the crusher of every foreign land, Tutꜥankhaten.*'

(iv) Upper arm [0·09], decorated zone with motifs $a$ - $a$ - $b_1$ - $a$ - $g_1$ - $f_1$ - $a$. In the centre, a broader zone, decorated with lozenge chequerboard, seven rows of light diamonds, six of dark. Then motifs $a$ - $f_1$ - $g_1$ - $a$ - $b_1$ - $a$. Colours: red, green [now very dark, almost black], and light brown barks, and gold leaf.

(v) Tip [0·04/0·05], plain dark red bark; the knob beyond the nock is covered with light brown bark. Nock: Plate xv.


**8**. Composite angular bow. Obj. no. 48 *j* (2); J.E. 61533; Exhib. no. 524 (identification confirmed by B.T. on the basis of the inscriptions). Description by Mace (two cards). 'Treated with melted paraffin wax' (Lucas). On display, CM, Room 30, case 109, top.

Provenience, as for **7**.

L., 1·13 (Mace); 1·135 (J.E.). Section elliptical; grip, 0·02 × 0·016; mid arm, 0·02 × 0·014; upper arm, 0·013 × 0·01; collar below nock, 0·014 × 0·014. Structure concealed by bark covering.

[1] The | of *ḥt* and *mry* restored; according to G.T.M., 'apparently blank, but wood warped, and possibly trace of matrix for | in both places'. [Ed.]

(i) Grip [0·12], plain light brown bark.

(ii) Lower arm [0·07], decorated zone [with motifs $a$ - $a$ - $b$ - $g_2$ - $a$]. In the centre, a band 0·02 wide, decorated with lozenge chequerboard: on a black ground, rows of light brown diamonds; on the intervening reserved black diamonds, small light brown dots [or small diamonds]. [Then motifs $a$ - $g_2$ - $b$ - $a$ - $a$.] Colours: black, dark red, light brown barks, with a few details in gold leaf.

(iii) Most of arm [0·33], plain light brown bark. On the face, a rectangular panel, 0·125 long, beginning 0·045 above zone (ii). In the panel, a hieroglyphic inscription in light brown bark, reading from tip to grip.

Inscription 8. 1 (Plate XVIII)

> '*The good god, the valiant, who acts with his (own) two arms, king of Upper and Lower Egypt, lord of the Two Lands, Nebkheprurēʿ, like Rēʿ.*'

Inscription 8. 2 (Plate XVIII)

> '*Son of Rēʿ, of his body, his beloved, lord of diadems, the protector of Egypt,*[1] *Tutʿankhaten.*'

(iv) Upper arm [0·09], decorated zone [with motifs $a$ - $a$ - $b$ - $g_1$ - $a$ - $f_2$; in the centre, a band decorated with lozenge chequerboard, as in zone (ii); then motifs $f_1$ - $a$ - $g_1$ - $b$ - $a$ - $a$]. Colours: black, dark red, green [now very dark, almost black], and light brown barks, with a few details in gold leaf.

(v) Tip [0·04], black bark; the knob beyond the nock covered with light brown bark.

**9.** Composite angular bow, elaborately decorated. Obj. no. 48 $k$ (1); J.E. 61526; Exhib. no. 121 (identification by CM, J.E.; confirmed by B.T. on the basis of the inscriptions). Photographs: whole bow, from side, Plate III; grip and lower arm, from back, Plate VI; tip, from side, Plate VII. Description by Mace (six cards). 'Sprayed with celluloid in amyl acetate; treated with melted paraffin wax' (Lucas). On display, CM, Room 30, case 75, no. 3.

Provenience, as for **1**. This bow was found with **10**, wrapped together in a strip of linen about 0·11 wide; one end of the cloth was turned down the bows, and then wound about them repeatedly, and fastened loosely with a knot at the other end.

L., 1·12 (Mace); 1·15 (emended from J.E., which gives 0·115). Section round at grip, 0·022 × 0·022; elliptical in mid arm, 0·02 × 0·015; upper arm, 0·013 × 0·01; collar below nock, 0·018 × 0·015. Structure concealed by bark covering.

(i) Grip [0·08], plain light brown bark.

(ii) Adjoining grip [0·045], decorated zone with motifs $a$ - $b_1$ - $h_2$ - $a$. In the centre, a band, 0·013 wide, which bears, on the face, two horses regarding each other, and on the back, a lozenge chequerboard of alternating dark and light diamonds, with smaller diamonds of a medium colour applied to the centre of each diamond. Then motifs $a$ - $h_1$ - $b_1$ - $a$. Colours: silver? (horses) [the horses are of dark red, outlined by light brown], dark red, green [now very dark, almost black], light brown, and gold.

(iii) Lower arm [0·015], decorated zone, bearing, on the sides, a plant design; on the back, a horse; on the face, a *sma* sign (symbolizing the 'Union of the Two Lands'), with a [negro] captive kneeling

---

[1] Reading *mki kmt.*

on each side of it, facing outwards, with one arm bound to the stem of the *sma*. Colours: black, dark red, green, light brown, and gold.

(iv) Lower arm [0·13/0·15], decorated inscribed zone; sides and back decorated with motifs $a$ - $b_1$ - $e$ - $g_2$ - $e$ - $b_1$; in the centre, a wider band, 0·05 wide, of light brown bark, bearing the vertical cartouches *Nebkheprurēʿ* and *Tutʿankhamūn*, with uraei; then motifs $a$ - $b_1$ - $i$ - $c$ - $b_1$ - $a$. On the face, a rectangular black panel, bearing a hieroglyphic inscription in light brown bark, reading from tip to grip.

### Inscription 9. 1 (Plate XVIII)

'*The good god, star[1] on the chariot, at whose rising* (literally, *when he rises*) *everyone lives,[2] the king of Upper and Lower Egypt, lord of the Two Lands, Nebkheprurēʿ, given life* (or, *may he be given life*).'

### Inscription 9. 2 (Plate XVIII)

'*The good god, vigorous in* (?) *his arm* (literally, *valiant upon* [or, *on account of*] *his arm*), *son of Rēʿ, of his body, his beloved, lord of diadems, Tutʿankhamūn—ruler-of-Southern-Heliopolis, like Rēʿ.*'

(v) Mid arm [0·015], a band of light brown; on it, on each side, a papyrus plant; on face and back, a horse. Colours: green [now very dark, almost black] and dark red.

(vi) Mid arm [0·02], inscribed band. On a black ground, a circumferent hieroglyphic inscription in light brown bark, its top towards the tip.

### Inscriptions 9. 3, 9. 4 (Plate XVIII)

'*The good god, Nebkheprurēʿ, son of Rēʿ, Tutʿankhamūn—ruler-of-Southern-Heliopolis.*'

(vii) Mid arm [0·015], horse and papyrus, as in zone (v).

(viii) Mid arm [0·12], decorated zone with motifs $a$ - $b_1$ - $h_2$ - $b_1$ - $a$ - $a$. In the centre, a band of light brown bark, 0·045, with vertical cartouches, *Nebkheprurēʿ* on the back, *Tutʿankhamūn* on the face. Then motifs $a$ - $e$ - $h_1$ - $a$ - $b_1$ - $a$. Colours: dark red, green [now very dark, almost black], light brown bark, gold leaf.

(ix) Upper arm [0·045], band of light brown bark, with vertical cartouches, *Nebkheprurēʿ* on the face, *Tutʿankhamūn* on the back, and uraei. Colours: silver and blue [no trace of these now], black, dark red, green [now very dark, almost black], and gold leaf.

(x) Upper arm [0·075], decorated zone with motifs $a$ - $b_1$ - $g_1$ - $a$ - $e$ - $a$. In the centre, a band of black bark, 0·015 wide, bearing circumferent cartouches in light brown bark, top towards tip, *Nebkheprurēʿ Tutʿankhamūn*: Inscriptions 9. 5, 9. 6 (Plate XVIII). Then motifs $a$ - $e$ - $a$ - $g_1$ - $b_1$ - $a$. Colours: dark red, black, light brown, green [now very dark, almost black], with a few details picked out in gold leaf.

(xi) Tip [0·055], feather or scale pattern, light brown on a dark red ground; bounded at the edge of the zone with three rings of gold leaf and two of green bark [now very dark, almost black]. The knob beyond the nock is covered with light brown bark. Nock: Plate XV.

---

[1] The reading ⋆| established by G.T.M.; for the epithet *sbꜣ ḥr ḥtr*, cf. *Urk.* IV. 1685. 1, 1723. 14: *sbꜣ n dʿm ssd.f ḥr ḥtr*. [Ed.]

[2] The restored reading ⚭[⚭ |] is owed to G.T.M. [Ed.

**10.** Composite angular bow. Obj. no. 48 *k* (2); J.E. 61523; Exhib. no. 522 (identification confirmed by B.T. on the basis of the inscriptions). Description by Mace (two cards). 'Sprayed with celluloid in amyl acetate; treated with melted paraffin wax' (Lucas). On display, CM, Room 30, case 75, no. 1.
  Provenience, as for **9**.

  L., 1·125 (Mace's notes and sketch); 1·315 (J.E.; probably an error for 1·125, which is wrongly ascribed to the following entry in J.E., the two lengths being interchanged). Section elliptical; grip 0·02 × 0·018; mid arm, 0·02 × 0·015; upper arm, 0·015 × 0·008; collar below nock, 0·015 × 0·015. Structure concealed by bark covering.

  (i) Grip and most of arm, plain light [yellowish] brown bark. On the face, a rectangular black panel, 0·17 long, beginning 0·095 from the centre of the grip; in the panel, a hieroglyphic inscription in light brown bark, reading from tip to grip.

Inscription 10. 1 (Plate XVIII)

> '*The good god, crusher of the (Nubian) bowmen, who beats the best of every foreign land, king of Upper and Lower Egypt, the subduer of the Nine Bows, lord of the Two Lands, Nebkheprurēꜥ.*'

Inscription 10. 2 (Plate XVIII)

> '*The good god, strong of bow, possessed of might, vigorous in drawing it, son of Rēꜥ, lord of diadems, Tutꜥankhamūn—ruler-of-Southern-Heliopolis, given life* (or, *may he be given life*) *like Rēꜥ.*'

  (ii) Tip [0·06], black bark; the knob beyond the nock is covered with light brown bark.


**11.** Composite angular bow. Obj. no. 77 *b*; J.E. 61519; Exhib. no. 3141 (identification by CM, PORTER–MOSS, I. ii², p. 581). Description by Mace (two cards). 'Treated with melted paraffin wax' (Lucas). In storage, CM, Tut. Magazine, box M.

  The Object number 77 is assigned to a pair of bows, one self and one composite, found on a cow-headed couch (Obj. no. 73) in the centre of the west wall of the Antechamber. The wooden bow is Obj. no. 77 *a* (Plate III).

  L., 1·25 (Mace); 1·26 (J.E.). Poor condition (J.E.). Section elliptical; grip, 0·028 × 0·02. Structure apparently concealed by bark covering. One of the surface strips covering the core must be broken, for Mace says: 'The bow was made of two pieces joined together, end of join coming 27 cm. from middle.'

  (i) Grip and lower arm [0·064], light yellow bark. On the face, rectangular panel of dark bark, 0·18 long, beginning 0·095 from the centre, and extending to 0·047 from the end of the zone. In the panel, a hieroglyphic inscription in light bark, reading from tip to grip.

Inscription 11. 1 (Plate XVIII)

> '*The good god, crushing the foreign land(s), lord of the Two Lands, master of the cultus, possessed of might, Nebkheprurēꜥ, given life* (or, *may he be given life*) *like Rēꜥ.*'

Inscription 11. 2 (Plate XVIII)

> '*Son of Rēꜥ, ruler of the Nine Bows, possessed of might, who assumes the white crown,*[1] *lord of diadems, Tutꜥankhamūn—ruler-of-Southern-Heliopolis, given life for ever* (or, *may he be given life for ever*).'

---

[1] The reading ⸶ ⸷ established by G.T.M.; for the transcription, cf. *Wb.* II. 262. 5–7. [Ed.]

(ii) Mid arm, 0·012, band of dark bark.

(iii) Upper arm [0·25], plain light yellow bark.

(iv) Tip, 0·04, plain dark bark. Nock: Plate xv.

**12.** Composite angular bow. Obj. no. 135 *z*; J.E. 61527; Exhib. no. 3110 (identification on basis of length, presence of titulary and banded grip, as specified in J.E.; confirmed by G.T.M.). Description by Mace (two cards). 'Treated with melted paraffin wax' (Lucas). In storage, CM, Tut. Magazine, box M.

The Object number 135 is assigned to a group of wooden staves found in the Antechamber, stacked carelessly together against the east wall, to the south of the entrance, behind three chariot wheels (Obj. nos. 133, 134, 136).

L. pr., 1·135 (Mace); 1·14 (emended from J.E., which gives 0·114). Poor condition (J.E.); nocks missing. Section elliptical; grip, 0·02 × 0·015; upper arm, 0·015 × 0·011. Details of structure largely concealed by bark covering; even so, Mace was able to distinguish the presence of one side strip, and a facing strip in the channel along the belly.

(i) Grip, 0·175, alternating bands of light and dark bark, each 0·006 wide.

(ii) Lower arm, 0·125, plain light bark. On the face, a dark panel, 0·07/0·072 long, beginning 0·055/0·05 from the grip; in the panel, a hieroglyphic inscription in light bark, reading from tip to grip.

Inscription 12. 1 (Plate XIX)

'*The good god, lord of the Two Lands, Nebkheprurēʿ, given life* (or, *may he be given life*).'

Inscription 12. 2 (Plate XIX)

'*Son of Rēʿ, lord of diadems, Tutʿankhamūn—ruler-of-Southern-Heliopolis, like Rēʿ.*'

(iii) Mid arm, 0·035, alternating bands of light and dark bark, each 0·003 wide.

(iv) Most of arm [0·22], plain light bark.

(v) Upper arm, 0·04, alternating bands of light bark and dark bark, each 0·003 wide in one arm; in the other arm, the light bands are 0·005 wide.

(vi) Tip, 0·055, plain dark bark.

**13.** Composite angular bow. Obj. no. 153; J.E. 61522; Exhib. no. 3117 (identification by CM, PORTER–MOSS, I. ii², p. 581). Description by Mace (two cards). 'Removed superficial dust; treated with melted paraffin wax' (Lucas). In storage, CM, Tut. Magazine, box M.

Object number 153, the bow, was found under a chariot (Obj. no. 121) in the Antechamber, about the middle of the south wall. Photograph of the chariot *in situ*, CARTER–MACE, I, pl. 26.

L., 1·085 (Mace); 1·09 (J.E.). Section nearly round, slightly flattened; diameter at grip, 0·02; at upper arm 0·013. Mace was able to distinguish a separate facing strip running the length of the stave. Bark covering attached with a dark resinous gum.

(i) Grip and lower arm [0·47], plain light brown bark. On the back (*sic*: face?), a rectangular panel of dark bark, 0·16 long [beginning 0·04 from centre and extending to 0·032 from the end of the zone]. In the panel, a hieroglyphic inscription in light bark, reading from tip to grip.

Inscription 13. 1 (Plate XIX)

> '*The good god, satisfied with truth, the maker of good laws throughout the entire land,*[1] *king of Upper and Lower Egypt, Nebkheprurēʿ.*'

Inscription 13. 2 (Plate XIX)

> '*The good god, great of strength, brawny armed, mighty of power, son of Rēʿ, lord of diadems, strong of bow, Tutʿankhamūn—ruler-of-Southern-Heliopolis.*'

(ii) Mid arm, 0·013, a band of dark bark.

(iii) Upper arm and tip, 0·295, plain light brown bark. Nock: Plate xv.

**14.** Composite angular bow, gold banded. Obj. no. 370 *ff*; probably J.E. 61528; probably Exhib. no. 3114 (identification on basis of decoration with two gold bands, specified in J.E.). Description, with section: McLeod, *JSA-A*, 7 (1964), p. 16, no. 1. Photographs: grip and lower arms, from side, Plate VIII; from face, Plate IX; tip, from side, Plate X. Description by Carter (two cards). Probably in storage, CM, Tut. Magazine, box M.

The Object number 370 is assigned to a large rough white wooden box, found in the Annexe, placed transversely across the chamber, at the south end opposite the doorway. The box is mentioned, CARTER–MACE, III, p. 127; *Treasure*, p. 33; picture *in situ*, CARTER–MACE, III, pl. 30*b*; cf. also ibid., III, pl. 31, where it has been set on the ground. The box contained an assortment of bows, arrows, clubs, and boomerangs; the bows are summarily described, ibid., III, pp. 138–41. The Annexe was cleared during the sixth season (1927/8).

L. when complete, est. 1·24 (Carter); l. pr., 1·215 (J.E.). One tip missing. Section in lower arm, 0·026×0·019. The facing strip at the grip has now sprung away from the core, thereby disclosing the structure.

The core is a wooden stave, 0·018×0·007 in the lower arm, running the length of the bowstave. It is flanked by wooden side strips, 0·004×0·009, bevelled so as to be almost triangular. The core is backed with a layer of 'gelatinous substance', 0·006 thick. It is faced with a lath of wood, 0·018×0·005, bevelled to an angle; this angle produces a keel along the face. Section: Plate XIV.

Enveloped in dark brown bark, like that from the cherry tree. A band of sheet gold [0·03 wide] encircles each arm some 0·25 from the centre. Otherwise undecorated. Nock: Plate xv.

**15.** Composite angular bow. Obj. no. 370 *gg*; J.E. 61521; Exhib. no. 3140 (identification, by CM, sent to Dr. Moss). Photographs: grip and lower arms, from side, Plate VIII; from face, Plate IX; tip, from side, Plate X. Description by Carter (one card). In storage, CM, Tut. Magazine, box M.

---

[1] For this epithet, cf. *Urk.* IV. 2061.4: *ir ḥpw nfrw*, and also the king's *nebty* name: *nfr ḥpw sgrḥ tȝwy*. It is perhaps the more meaningful in the light of Tutʿankhamūn's widely publicized reforms; cf. the 'Restoration' inscription: P. Lacau, *Stèles du nouvel empire*, 1 (Cairo, 1909), pl. 70; *Urk.* IV. 2025 ff.; J. Bennett, *JEA*, 25 (1939), pp. 8 ff.

Provenience, as for **14**.

L. when complete, est. 1·14 (Carter); l. pr., 1·12 (J.E.). One tip missing. Section at grip almost round: diameter, 0·023. Piece of string adhering to one nock. Carter does not give details of structure, only specifying that it resembles that of **14**; presumably, that is, wooden core, facing, and side-strips, with a backing of a 'gelatinous substance'. Covered with bark.

(i) Grip [0·16], plain light bark, resembling birch.

(ii) Lower arm [0·035], decorated zone with motifs $a - b_1 - e - g_1 - e - b_1 - a$.

(iii) Lower arm [0·155], plain light bark. On the face, a dark rectangular panel [0·11 long, beginning 0·03 from zone (ii)]. On the face, between the bottom of the panel and the end of the zone, a horse and fan. In the panel, a hieroglyphic inscription in light bark, reading from tip to grip, and framed by symbols for gold and myriads of years.

Inscription 15. 1 (Plate IX; Plate XIX)

'*The good god, strong of bow, possessed of might, vigorous in drawing it, lord of the Two Lands, Nebkheprurēʿ.*'

Inscription 15. 2 (Plate IX; Plate XIX)

'*Son of Rēʿ, of his body, his beloved, lord of diadems, smiting the Nine Bows, lord of every foreign land, Tutʿankhamūn—ruler-of-Southern-Heliopolis.*'

(iv) Mid arm [0·03], dark band, with border of multiple light strips, bearing circumferent cartouches, top towards tip, *Nebkheprurēʿ Tutʿankhamūn*.[1]

(v) Upper arm [*c.* 0·17], plain light bark.

(vi) Upper arm [0·035], dark band bearing similar circumferent cartouches, with border of motif *a* enclosed by a triple light strip.

(vii) Tip [0·06], plain light bark. Nock: Plate XV.


**16.** Composite angular bow. Obj. no. 370 *hh*; probably J.E. 61534; probably Exhib. no. 3116 (identification on basis of double zigzag motif, mentioned in J.E.). According to J.E., this is the bow cited: A. Lucas, 'Notes on Some of the Objects from the Tomb of Tut-ankhamun', *ASAE*, 41 (1942), p. 144; LUCAS–HARRIS, pp. 429, 430, 431. Photographs: grip and lower arms, from side, Plate VIII; from face, Plate IX; tip, from side, Plate X. Description by Carter (one card). Part of the bow used for botanical analysis. Probably in storage, CM, Tut. Magazine, box M.

Provenience, as for **14**.

L. when complete, est. 1·16 (Carter)—one tip missing when discovered; l. pr. after analysis, 1·02+? (J.E.). Section at grip almost round, 0·022 [×0·02]. Carter does not give details of its structure, remarking only that it was similar to that of **14**; presumably, that is, wooden core, facing, and side-strips, with a backing of a 'gelatinous substance'. Covered with bark.

In 1933, after the bow had reached Cairo, Lucas submitted a sample to Dr. Laurence Chalk, Imperial Forestry Institute, Oxford. He identified the wood as ash (*Fraxinus* sp.), probably not the manna ash (*F. ornus*).[2]

---

[1] Cf. Inscriptions 9. 5, 9. 6, with similar disposition of signs in the prenomen (see Plate IX). [Ed.]

[2] Letter of 17 January 1934 (copy on file in the Commonwealth Forestry Institute, Oxford; reference W. 78 b).

I am grateful to J. F. Hughes of the Institute for sending me the records of the identification. Lucas had given the number 15/33 to the sample; he describes it only as 'the long piece with a slight curve'.

(i) Grip [0·12], alternating bands of light and dark bark, nine of each, 0·006 wide.

(ii) Lower arm [0·035], decorated zone, with motifs $a$ - $b_1$ (?); in the centre, a wider band [about 0·01 wide], decorated with a chequerboard motif, eight rows of alternating dark and light squares; then motifs $b_1$ (?) - $a$.

(iii) Lower arm [0·13], plain dark reddish brown bark, resembling cherry. On the face, a dark rectangular panel [0·085 long, beginning 0·035 from the lower end of the zone, and extending to 0·01 from the upper end of the zone]. In the panel, a double overlapping zigzag.

(iv) Mid arm [0·02], dark band, bearing the king's cartouches.

(v) Upper arm [c. 0·20], plain dark reddish brown bark.

(vi) Upper arm [0·05], decorated zone with motifs $a$ - $b_1$; in the centre, a wider band decorated with a square chequerboard, as in zone (ii); then motifs $b_1$ - $a$.

(vii) Tip [0·07], plain dark reddish brown bark. Nock: Plate xv.

17. Composite angular bow, undecorated. Obj. no. 370 *ii*; J.E. 61530; Exhib. no. 1600 (identification confirmed by B.T. on the basis of Burton's photographs). Description, with section: McLeod, *JSA-A*, 7 (1964), pp. 16–17, no. 2. Photographs: grip and lower arms, from side, Plate VIII; from face, Plate IX; tip, from side, Plate x. Description by Carter (one card). On display, CM, Room 30, case 75, no. 7.

Provenience, as for 14.

L., 1·11 (Carter); 1·125 (J.E.). String still adheres to one nock. Grip contracted, with circumferent grooves or lines on the grip. In structure the bow resembles 14, that is, a wooden core, facing strip, and side strips, and a backing of a 'gelatinous substance'. But there is a significant difference. The constituent parts in the grip are shaped differently from those in the arm. The grip [0·11 long], is oval in section, 0·019 wide, while the arms are flatter, 0·025 wide, with thicker side strips, bevelled to an angle. Sections: Plate XIV.

Covered with a birch-like bark. [Quite a bit of this has now come off, revealing polished dark reddish brown wood beneath it.] Undecorated. Nock: Plate xv.

18. Composite bow. Obj. no. 370 *jj*. On identity and present location, see page 26. Description by Carter (one card).

Provenience, as for 14.

Length, 'similar to' that of 17 (i.e. about 1·11). One tip missing. No information about profile. 'Similar to' 17; probably in structure; presumably, that is, wooden core, facing, and side strips, with a backing of a 'gelatinous substance'; probably in decoration (i.e. undecorated).

19. Short composite angular bow. Obj. no. 370 *kk*; J.E. 61538; Exhib. no. 1598 (identification, by CM, PORTER–MOSS, I, ii², p. 581). Description by Carter (one card). On display CM, Room 30, case 109, extreme right.

Provenience, as for 14.

L., 0·72 (Carter and J.E.). Section flattened, with back flat, face rounded (Plate XIV). Width, 0·015. Structure concealed by bark covering (Carter says, 'made entirely of self wood').

(i) Grip and most of arm, covered with a birch-like bark. On the face, near grip, a rectangular panel, bearing a hieroglyphic inscription.

Inscription 19. 1 (Plate XIX)

'*The good god, lord of the Two Lands, Nebkheprurēᶜ, strong of bow.*'

Inscription 19. 2 (Plate XIX)

'*Son of Rēᶜ, of [his] body, [his] beloved,*[1] *Tutᶜankhamūn—ruler-of-Southern-Heliopolis, like Rēᶜ.*'[2]

(ii) Tip, 0·02, covered with dark red bark, resembling cherry.

**20.** Miniature composite angular bow. Obj. no. 370 *ll*; probably J.E. 61543; probably Exhib. no. 930 (identification on basis of length—0·3 shorter than any other). Description by Carter (one card). Probably on display CM, Room 30, case 75, no. 10.

Provenience, as for **14.**

L., 0·34 (Carter); 0·342 (J.E.); width at grip 0·011.

[Profile angular, with slight angle at grip; much less curvature than any other composite bow on display]. Carter notes that a line joining the tips would touch the grip. Undecorated. [Plain dark bark].

This bow has been called a toy (J. Leibovitch, *Ancient Egypt*, tr. A. Rowe [Cairo, 1938], p. 148), and this is probably true in some sense. But bows no larger than this—self bows, admittedly—are common in equatorial and southern Africa as well as elsewhere.[3] The possibility remains then that this bow was experimental, and was intended for something more than a child's bow.

**21.** Short composite angular bow. Obj. no. 596 *k*; probably J.E. 61532; probably Exhib. no. 1596 (identification tentatively confirmed by B.T. on the basis of Carter's notes). Description, with cross-section: McLeod, *JSA-A*, 7 (1964), p. 17, no. 3. Photograph: whole bow, from side, Plate XI. Description by Carter (one card). Probably on display, CM, Room 30, case 109, second from left.

The Object number 596 is assigned to a bundle of fans, sticks, bows, and arrows found in the Annexe, cast on top of the miscellanea under the bed (Obj. no. 377) at the south end of the chamber. Its position is marked in CARTER–MACE, III, pl. 31, by the label 596 in the centre background. The Annexe was cleared during the sixth season (1927/8).

L., 1·02 (Carter and J.E.). Section, probably in lower arm [0·025 × 0·012]. The structure is comparatively simple. The core, a thin stave of wood [0·025 × 0·004], is backed with a layer [0·002 thick] of a 'gelatinous substance', and faced with a thicker layer [maximum, 0·006] of the same material, moulded to produce a keel. Section: Plate XIV.

(i) Grip and most of arm, covered with a light yellowish birch-like bark. On the face, a rectangular panel of dark brown bark.

---

[1] Understand *n ḫt⟨.f⟩ mry⟨.f⟩*.

[2] Taking the faulty writing as a mistake for *mi rᶜ* (rather than *di ᶜnḫ*); see note on Inscription 1. 2, above. [Ed.]

[3] Examples of miniature bows which were capable of effective use include Oxford, Pitt Rivers Museum, J. S. Jameson Collection, labelled 'd.d. Mrs. MacDonnell, 1927' (Congo Pygmy-type bow; *c.* 35 cm. from tip to tip when strung); British Museum, Trobriand Islands, labelled '1950. Oc. 2. 116' (wood, self bow; *c.* 35 cm. when strung); Royal Ontario Museum, Cat. no. HA–551 (Bushman bow; 20 cm. when strung); on the ten-centimetre 'Bushman revolver', see I. Schapera, 'Bows and Arrows of the Bushman', *Man*, 27 (1927), pp. 113–17, esp. 116–17.

(ii) Tip [0·04], dark brown bark; the knob beyond the nock covered with light yellow bark. Nock: Plate xv.

**22.** Short composite angular bow. Obj. no. 596 *l*; probably J.E. 61536; probably Exhib. no. 1601 (identification tentatively suggested on basis of length; tentatively confirmed by B.T. on basis of presence of gilt decoration). Description by Carter (part card). Probably on display, CM, Room 30, case 109, second from right.

Provenience, as for **21**.

L., 0·98 m. (Carter and J.E.). Similar in structure to **21**; presumably, that is, a flat wooden core, with facing and backing of a 'gelatinous substance'. Decoration similar to **21**, except that the rectangular [black] panel on the face of each arm is decorated with a gilt pattern [two rows of large four-pointed stars, alternating with three rows of small diamonds].

**23.** Short composite angular bow. Obj. no. 596 *m*; probably J.E. 61531; probably Exhib. no. 1597 (identification tentatively confirmed by B.T. on the basis of Carter's notes). Description by Carter (part card). Probably on display, CM, Room 30, case 109, extreme left.

Provenience, as for **21**.

L., 0·885 (Carter); 0·875 (J.E.). Broken. Structure similar to **21**; presumably, that is, a flat wooden core with facing and backing of a 'gelatinous substance'.

(i) Grip and most of arm, covered with a light yellowish bark, resembling silver birch; much lighter [not so much; a little lighter] than the bark of **21**—Naples yellow. On the face, a dark rectangular panel, uncharged.

(ii) Tip [covered with dark brown bark].

**24.** Short composite bow. Obj. no. 596 *n*. On identity and present location, see page 26. Description by Carter (part card).

Provenience, as for **21**.

L., 0·69 (Carter). No information on profile. Similar in structure to **21**; presumably, that is, a flat wooden core, with facing and backing of a 'gelatinous substance'. Bark decoration on face, at mid arm, probably in the form of a panel. Bark decoration at tips.

**25.** Short composite bow. Obj. no. 596 *o*. On identity and present location, see page 26. Description by Carter (part card).

Provenience, as for **21**.

L., 0·74 (Carter). Broken. No information on profile. Similar in structure to **21**; presumably, that is, a flat wooden core, with facing and backing of a 'gelatinous substance'. Bark decoration on lower arms, adjoining grip. Bark decoration at tips.

**26.** Short composite angular bow. Obj. no. 596 $p$; J.E. 61542; Exhib. no. 929 (identification on basis of length—no other bow comes within 0·06 of this; confirmed by B.T.'s description, which coincides fully with the detail of Burton's photograph). Photograph: whole bow, from side, Plate XI. Description by Carter (part card). On display, CM, Room 30, case 75, no. 9.

Provenience, as for **21**.

L., 0·635 (Carter); 0·64 (J.E.). Similar in structure to **21**; presumably, that is, a flat wooden core, with facing and backing of a 'gelatinous substance'.

(i) Centre of grip [0·03], plain light bark.

(ii) Edge of grip [0·01/0·015], decorated zone; [band of dark red bark, overlaid near each edge by three narrow strips of yellow bark].

(iii) Arm [0·25], plain light bark; [on the face, at mid arm, a rectangular dark panel in one arm; a similar panel, lighter in colour, in the other arm].

(iv) Tip [0·025], dark bark; the knob beyond the nock is light in colour.


**27.** Short composite angular bow, elaborately decorated. Obj. no. 596 $q$; J.E. 61518; Exhib. no. 1599 (identification by B.T. on the basis of Burton's photograph). Photographs: whole bow, from side, Plate XI; grip and lower arm, from face, Plate XII. Description by Carter (part card). On display, CM, Room 30, case 75, no. 8.

Provenience, as for **21**.

L., 1·03 (Carter); 1·04 (J.E.). Similar in structure to **21**; presumably, that is, a flat wooden core, with facing and backing of a 'gelatinous substance'. The photograph shows a keel along the face.

(i) Grip [0·085], plain light bark.

(ii) Lower arm [0·065], decorated zone with motifs $a$ - $a$ - $e$ - $e$ - $b_2$ - $g_1$ - $a$ - $c$ - $a$ - $a$.

(iii) Lower arm [0·035], dark zone, decorated on the face with a light-coloured plumed horse above two fans.

(iv) Lower arm [0·065], decorated zone with motifs $a$ - $a$ - $c$ - $g_1$ - $a$ - $b_2$ - $a$ - $d$ - $a$ - $a$.

(v) Lower arm [0·035], light zone, decorated on the face with a wild goat, outlined in dark, over an eight-stemmed bush.

(vi) Mid arm [0·15], plain light bark; on the face, a rectangular panel, filled with a rhombic chequerboard: four rows of light diamonds, separated by dark diamonds.

(vii) Tip [0·13], decorated zone; details not available.


**28.** Short composite angular bow, elaborately decorated. Obj. no. 596 $r$; probably J.E. 61539; probably Exhib. no. 3112 (tentative identification on basis of length, and presence of decorative motifs $d$ and $f$ or $g$, which are mentioned in J.E.). Photographs: whole bow, from side, Plate XI; grip and lower arm, from face, Plate XII. Description by Carter (part card). Probably in storage, CM, Tut. Magazine, box M.

Provenience, as for **21**.

L., 0·905 (Carter); 0·91 (J.E.). Similar in structure to **21**; presumably, that is, a flat wooden core, with facing and backing of a 'gelatinous substance'. The photograph shows a keel along the face.

E

(i) Grip [0·12], plain light bark.

(ii) Lower arm [0·12], decorated zone with motifs $a$ - $b_1$ - $g_1$ - $c$ - $d$; then a broader band [0·025], apparently of dark bark, decorated with an unidentified charge; then motifs $d$ - $c$ - $g_1$ - $b_1$ - $a$.

(iii) Most of arm, plain light bark; on the face, a long rectangular dark panel [beginning 0·035 from the lower end of the zone]. Between the panel and the end of the zone, on the face, a dark seven-leafed palmette.

(iv) Tip: details not available.

**29.** Short composite angular bow. Obj. no. 596 $s$; probably J.E. 61535; probably Exhib. no. 3115 (tentative identification on basis of length, and presence of sun-burst palmette as decorative motif, specified in J.E.). Description, with section: McLeod, *JSA-A*, 7 (1964), p. 17, no. 4. Photographs: whole bow, from side, Plate XI; grip and lower arm, from face, Plate XII. Description by Carter (one card). Probably in storage, CM, Tut. Magazine, box M.

Provenience, as for **21**.

L., 0·925 (Carter); 0·93 (J.E.). Bad condition (J.E.). Grip approximately oval [0·015 × 0·011]; limbs near grip broadened and flattened [0·02 × 0·009]. Keel along face.

The section is unusual. Running the length of the bow are four thin strips of hard wood [each 0·002 thick], perpendicular to the back; between these strips, and outside them, are layers of a 'gelatinous substance', of about the same thickness. Section: Plate XIV. The grip is still sheathed in bark; but the intact sheath and the contracted grip both suggest that it is of solid wood.

Covered with a bark resembling birch, with a few decorations in darker bark.

(i) Grip [0·16], undecorated.

(ii) Narrow dark band [0·013], bearing a seven-leafed sun-burst palmette outlined in light.

(iii) Triangular panel [maximum, 0·011], terminating on the face in an angle pointing towards tip.

(iv) Arm, apparently undecorated.

(v) Tip: one tip is plain bark, the other gilt.

## Correlation with Museum Numbers

In the foregoing catalogue Museum numbers are included for most entries. Three of the bows remain unidentified, **18, 24, 25**. I am grateful for the opportunity to present details of these unidentified bows from the *Journal d'Entrée du Musée*.

| J.E. 61529 | Exhib. no. 3111 | In storage, Tut. Mag., box M | L., 1·07 | Bow, composite; no inscription; banded decoration at grip | Probably **18.** 370 $jj$ |
| J.E. 61540 | Exhib. no. 3109 | In storage, Tut. Mag., box M | L., 0·70 | Bow, composite; plain panel decoration only | Probably **24.** 596 $n$ **25.** 596 $o$ |
| J.E. 61541 | Exhib. no. 3108 | In storage, Tut. Mag., box M | L., 0·71 | Bow, composite (small); chequerboard decoration | |

It may be convenient to append a full list of the composite bows from the tomb, in the order of their listing in the J.E.

| | | | | |
|---|---|---|---|---|
| J.E. 61517 | Exhib. no. 120 | 4 | 48 *h* | certain |
| J.E. 61518 | Exhib. no. 1599 | 27 | 596 *q* | certain |
| J.E. 61519 | Exhib. no. 3141 | 11 | 77 *b* | certain |
| J.E. 61520 | Exhib. no. 3113 | 3 | 48 *g* (2) | certain |
| J.E. 61521 | Exhib. no. 3140 | 15 | 370 *gg* | certain |
| J.E. 61522 | Exhib. no. 3117 | 13 | 153 | certain |
| J.E. 61523 | Exhib. no. 522 | 10 | 48 *k* (2) | certain |
| J.E. 61524 | Exhib. no. 523 | 2 | 48 *g* (1) | certain |
| J.E. 61525 | Exhib. no. 128 | 7 | 48 *j* (1) | certain |
| J.E. 61526 | Exhib. no. 121 | 9 | 48 *k* (1) | certain |
| J.E. 61527 | Exhib. no. 3110 | 12 | 135 *z* | certain |
| J.E. 61528 | Exhib. no. 3114 | 14 | 370 *ff* | probable |
| J.E. 61529 | Exhib. no. 3111 | | | uncertain: see above |
| J.E. 61530 | Exhib. no. 1600 | 17 | 370 *ii* | certain |
| J.E. 61531 | Exhib. no. 1597 | 23 | 596 *m* | probable |
| J.E. 61532 | Exhib. no. 1596 | 21 | 596 *k* | probable |
| J.E. 61533 | Exhib. no. 524 | 8 | 48 *j* (2) | certain |
| J.E. 61534 | Exhib. no. 3116 | 16 | 370 *hh* | probable |
| J.E. 61535 | Exhib. no. 3115 | 29 | 596 *s* | probable |
| J.E. 61536 | Exhib. no. 1601 | 22 | 596 *l* | probable |
| J.E. 61537 | Exhib. no. 119 | 6 | 48 *i* (2) | certain |
| J.E. 61538 | Exhib. no. 1598 | 19 | 370 *kk* | certain |
| J.E. 61539 | Exhib. no. 3112 | 28 | 596 *r* | probable |
| J.E. 61540 | Exhib. no. 3109 | | | uncertain: see above |
| J.E. 61541 | Exhib. no. 3108 | | | uncertain: see above |
| J.E. 61542 | Exhib. no. 929 | 26 | 596 *p* | certain |
| J.E. 61543 | Exhib. no. 930 | 20 | 370 *ll* | probable |
| J.E. 61544 | Exhib. no. 127 | 5 | 48 *i* (1) | certain |
| J.E. 61545 | Exhib. no. 520 | 1 | 48 *f* | certain |

## COMPOSITE BOWS NOT DESCRIBED IN CARTER'S NOTES

**30–2 (?).** Three composite bows; Obj. no. 335 *a*. In the fifth season (1926/7), Carter found a beautiful bow-case (Obj. no. 335), leaning against the north-west corner of the Treasury; it was decorated with fine marquetry, depicting the young pharaoh in the hunt.[1] According to the preliminary publication, this bow-case contained 'three neatly made composite bows, now, unfortunately, in a parlous condition, their gelatinous cores at some early period having become viscid, with the result that they leaked out, and dried into a solid black mass' (CARTER–MACE, III, p. 95). At the time of finding, the case was not shut, and the tip of one bow protruded; it can be seen in the photograph, CARTER–MACE, III, pl. 4*a*.

[1] Mentioned: CARTER–MACE, III, p. 34; *Treasure*, p. 28; described: CARTER–MACE, III, pp. 94–6; pictures: ibid., III, pls. 4*a*, 28, 29; *Treasure*, pl. 52; text of inscriptions (incomplete): *Urk.* IV. 2057.15–2059.8; translated: *Übersetzung*, pp. 379–80.

There is no further record of these bows. In Carter's field-notes on the bow-case there is an annotation 'For contents see 335 *a*'; but there is no card numbered 335 *a*.

**33** (?). Several fragments of composite bows were employed for analysis, according to notes on file in the Griffith Institute (see below, pages 31–2). They cannot be identified with any of the complete bows catalogued so far.

# MORPHOLOGICAL COMMENTARY

### COMPARATIVE MATERIAL

(**A**) New York, Metropolitan Museum of Art, Acc. no. 28. 9. 9; found at Thebes in 1906/7 by the Earl of Carnarvon, at the site of a tomb in the ʿAsâsîf which was perhaps of the Seventeenth Dynasty, but which certainly antedated the temple of Hatshepsut. Description: McLeod, *AJA*, 66 (1962), pp. 15–16, no. 1. Section: Plate XIV; nock: Plate XV.

(**B, C**) New York, Metropolitan Museum of Art, Acc. no. 25. 3. 303; fragments of two bows, found at Thebes in 1921/2 by H. E. Winlock, in grave pit 1013 of the Sʿankhkarēʿ cemetery, the tomb of ʿAḥmose Penḥut, 'attendant and fan-bearer' of Tuthmosis I (PORTER–MOSS, I. ii², p. 668). Description: McLeod, *AJA*, 66 (1962), pp. 16–17, nos. 2, 3. Sections: Plate XIV.

(**D**) New York, Metropolitan Museum of Art, Acc. no. 25. 3. 304; found at Thebes in 1920/1, in the rubbish on the Sʿankhkarēʿ temple platform; presumably contemporary with **B, C**, above. Description: McLeod, *AJA*, 66 (1962), pp. 17–18, no. 4. Section: Plate XIV.

(**E**) Cairo, Egyptian Museum, J.E. 31389; found at Thebes in 1896 by G. Daressy, in a rock-cut tomb in Draʿ Abû el-Nagaʿ (PORTER–MOSS, I. ii², p. 614); the tomb belonged to Se-aa (*s-ʿ₃*), apparently 'Se-aa the Palestinian (Kharu)', who died either in the latter part of the reign of Tuthmosis III, or under Amenophis II. Noted: G. Daressy, *Rec Trav*, 20 (1898), p. 73; G. A. Wainwright, *Bull. Soc. sultanieh de géog.*, 9 (1919), p. 114; G. Brunton, *ASAE*, 38 (1938), pp. 251–2; LUCAS–HARRIS, p. 29. Section: Plate XIV.

(**F**) Cairo, Egyptian Museum, J.E. 32612; found at Thebes in 1898 by V. Loret, in the tomb of Amenophis II, in the Valley of the Kings (PORTER–MOSS, I. ii², p. 556). Description: G. Daressy, *Fouilles de la Vallée des Rois* (Cairo, 1902), pp. 68–9, no. 24120; further details noted: N. de G. Davies, *BMMA*, 30 (1935), *Egyptian Exped. 1934–1935*, p. 50; McLeod, *AJA*, 66 (1962), p. 14, n. 19. Improved text of inscriptions: *Urk.* IV. 1363. 4–20; translated: *Übersetzung*, pp. 60–1, no. 400 (2). Section: Plate XIV.

(**G**) Berlin, Staatliche Museen, Aegyptische Abteilung, Inv. nr. 4712; formerly Passalacqua Collection, no. 566; found at Thebes in 1822/5 by Giuseppe Passalacqua, in a re-used Eleventh Dynasty corridor tomb on the southern spur of Draʿ Abû el-Nagaʿ; associated with a burial contemporary with Ramesses II (PORTER–MOSS, I. ii², p. 612). Description: F. von Luschan, *ZfE*, 25 (1893), Beibl., pp. 266–71. Section: Plate XIV.

(**H**) Oxford, Pitt Rivers Museum, labelled 'd.d. H. Balfour, Jan. 1896'; found at Thebes about 1877, by Arminius Butros, Italian consular agent, allegedly in a Twenty-sixth Dynasty Tomb. Description: H. Balfour, *JRAI*, 26 (1896/7), pp. 210–20. Section: Plate xiv.

(**I**) New York, Brooklyn Museum, Acc. no. 37. 1835E; formerly Abbott Collection, no. 421. 1A; found at Saqqâra in 1832/43 by Henry Abbott, M.D. Undated. Description: McLeod, *AJA*, 62 (1958), pp. 397–401. Section: Plate xiv.

(**J**) Cairo, Egyptian Museum, T(emporary) R(eference) or Prov(isional) no. $\dfrac{21}{23}\bigg|\dfrac{1}{1}$; Fiche de Maspero ('Old Number') 4725. Provenience and date unknown. Noted: Wreszinski, *Atlas*, 1, pl. 80, n. 4; P. Thomsen, *Ebert's Reallexikon der Vorgeschichte*, 2 (Berlin, 1925), p. 52; E. Robinson, *Archery*, 23. 4 (April, 1951), p. 5.

### Length

On the basis of their lengths, extant examples of ancient Egyptian composite bows fall into fairly well-defined groups:

| L. (metres) | | |
|---|---|---|
| 1·31–1·40 | **A, E, H, I, J,** | **2, 4, 5** |
| 1·19–1·26 | **C, G,** | **3, 6, 11, 14** |
| 1·07–1·16 | | **1, 7, 8, 9, 10, 12, 13, 15, 16, 17, 18** |
| 0·98–1·04 | | **21, 22, 27** |
| 0·87–0·93 | | **23, 28, 29** |
| 0·69–0·74 | | **19, 24, 25** |
| *c.* 0·64 | | **26** |
| *c.* 0·34 | | **20** |

Of the seven longest, only two are from the tomb: and these are the exceptional 'captive' bow (**5**) and the unique 'Bow of Honour' (**4**). The twenty-three shortest bows known are all from the tomb.

For comparison the typical ancient Scythian composite bow measured 0·75 or less when strung;[1] an ancient composite of Persian type measured 1·275 from tip to tip;[2] the Turkish bow almost never exceeds 1·17 along the curve; modern Persian, Indian, and Chinese composite bows are usually between 1·20 and 1·50 when strung.[3]

These lengths are substantially shorter than the longest self bows. Ancient Egyptian wooden bows of 1·70 are not rare; three specimens from the tomb of Tutʿankhamūn exceeded 1·90—the length of the mediaeval English long-bow.

It is possible that the smaller composite bows from the tomb had belonged to the king as a child. Nos. **19–29**, the shortest specimens in the catalogue, were found together in two groups in the

---

[1] F. E. Brown, *SemKond*, 9 (1937), p. 7; W. McLeod, *Greek Heritage*, 1. 3 (1964), p. 107. The most recent discussion is A. I. Melyukova, *Vooruzhenie Skifov: Scythian Weapons* (in the series *Arkheologiya SSSR: svod arkheologicheskikh istochnikov*, Moscow, 1964), pp. 14–15: most of the evidence indicates a length of 0 60–0·70, but some examples were half as long again.

[2] F. E. Brown, *SemKond*, 9 (1937), p. 1.

[3] R. Payne-Gallwey, *The Turkish Composite Bow*, Appendix to *The Crossbow*, p. 3.

Annexe, which also held a number of other possessions which had been his as a child.[1] One of them (19) bears the king's name in the form Tut'ankhamūn, rather than in the original form Tut'ankhaten.

## PROFILE

Normally ancient Egyptian composite bows are angular, bent at the grip (**B, C, D, E, G, H, I, J**). There is a single aberrant example: the bow of Amenophis II (**F**), a 'one-curve composite' (*AJA*, 66 [1962], p. 14, n. 19).

Of the Tut'ankhamūn bows, fifteen are sketched in profile on the inventory cards by Mace or Carter; all are angular (**1–14, 21**). Burton's photographs show the profile of fourteen; all are angular (Plates III, VIII, XI; **1, 4, 5, 7, 9, 14–17, 21, 26–9**). Seventeen are on display in Cairo—all angular (**1, 2, 4–10, 17, 19, 26, 27**, and probably **20–3**). Thus twenty-six bows from the tomb are unquestionably angular; for the others, there is no information.

## MATERIALS

The typical composite bow consists of a wooden core, with a layer of sinew applied to the back, and a layer of horn on the face; the whole bow is usually covered by a protective bark sheath. It seems likely that in general the Tut'ankhamūn bows adhered to this scheme.

The wood of one bow (probably **16**) was identified by Dr. Laurence Chalk, Imperial Forestry Institute, Oxford, as ash (*Fraxinus* sp.), probably not manna ash (*F. ornus*). Carter had also submitted specimens of 'wood and bark decoration from composite bows' to L. A. Boodle, Royal Botanic Gardens, Kew; the fragments analysed were unnumbered, but there is no reason to assume that they came from the same bow as the sample submitted to Chalk by Lucas. Boodle identified the wood as flowering or manna ash (*F. ornus*).[2]

The bark covering of several bows (**15, 17, 19, 21, 23, 29**) was tentatively identified by Carter as birch; on three other bows he hesitantly describes it as 'cherry-like' (**14, 16, 19**). These are doubtless intelligent guesses, and inevitably carry less authority than expert botanical testimony (cf. CARTER–MACE, III, p. 138).

Carter's notes mention neither sinew nor horn. They do describe one constituent of four bows (**14, 17, 21, 29**; probably also **15, 16, 18, 22–8**) as a 'gelatinous substance'. In three (**14, 17, 21**; probably also **15, 16, 18, 22–8**) it was found along the back, where one would normally expect sinew; possibly it is the end-product of the degeneration of sinew. It is known that if certain animal products are 'exposed to excess of water for a lengthy period of time, a complete breakdown of structure will take place by the chemical action known as hydrolysis: the proteins are degraded,

---

[1] e.g. nursery chair, CARTER–MACE, III, p. 113; child's footstools, ibid., III, p. 115; 'the linen chests of His Majesty, when he was a youth', ibid., III, p. 119; a chest of playthings, ibid., III, pp. 120–3; a falchion, 'probably made for the king when a child', ibid., III, p. 137. *Contra*, cf. royal clothing of the boy-king, and a docket reading 'the king's side-lock (?) as a boy', found in the Antechamber, CARTER–MACE, I, p. 172; child's chair, Obj. no. 39, ibid., I pl. 59.

[For the dockets, see now J. Černý, *Hieratic Inscriptions from the Tomb of Tut'ankhamūn* (Tomb Series, II), Oxford,

1965. The 'linen chests' are in fact Obj. nos. 493 (+494), 594 (+575) = Černý Inscr. nos. 57, 59; the 'side-lock (?)' would appear to refer (incorrectly) to the docket on Obj. no. 68 = Černý Inscr. no. 50. A loose docket from the Annexe, Obj. no. 620 (96) = Černý Inscr. no. 63, also relates to possessions of His Majesty '*when he was a boy*'.] [Ed.]

[2] Letter of 7 September 1932 (on file in the Griffith Institute); cf. also his letter of 31 May 1932 ('ash'); and the final report he prepared for Carter.

the organized structures disappear, and a form of gelatine results'.[1] This change is best attested for parchment. But Carter likewise observed that much of the leather in Tutʿankhamūn's tomb had been 'melted', as he called it, by the heat and dampness (CARTER–MACE, I, pp. 121, 170; II, p. 55; III, p. 151; cf. II, pp. 175–6). Moreover, he described how parts of three other bows (30–2) 'at some early period [had] become viscid, with the result that they leaked out, and dried into a black solid mass' (CARTER–MACE, III, p. 95). I have consulted Professor C. S. Hanes, F.R.S., head of the Department of Biochemistry in the University of Toronto; in his opinion the proteins of animal sinew might well undergo a similar hydrolysis, if stored in a sufficiently humid atmosphere for a sufficiently long time.

The absence of horn from the four bows specifically described by Carter (14, 17, 21, 29) requires comment. There are three possible explanations, none of them free of difficulties. (1) Horn was not used in the bows. For the group as a whole this is unlikely, since the structure of the bows would then be anomalous. (This argument does not apply to individual weapons. Among the pieces studied by Lucas was a 'section of compound bow [620]'. His notes identify the material as 'probably thick hide, rhinoceros or hippopotamus'—presumably a substitute for horn.) (2) Horn *was* used, but has, like the sinew, been subjected to hydrolysis. Professor Hanes inclines to believe that, under suitable conditions, the protein in horn might also be hydrolysed. The chief obstacle is that the tomb included horn which had not deteriorated (Obj. no. 92 *e*—apparently the ibex horn which has now been inserted in Obj. no. 584, the calcite vase in the form of an ibex; Obj. no. 578, calcite pedestal and boat, terminating in ibex figureheads, with real horns; Obj. no. 585 *m*, horn bracelet). (3) Horn was used, and is still present in the bows; but Carter mistook it for wood. Carter's notes certainly specify the presence of wood along the face, where one would expect horn, in 14, 17. On balance, this is the least unlikely explanation. It is favoured by the *Journal d'Entrée du Musée*, which describes the material of all these bows as 'wood, *horn*, linen, bark'. It seems also to be confirmed by Boodle's analysis, for he reported that a number of fragments of 'wood' from composite bows sent to him by Carter were in fact horn.

The notes on 13 specify the presence of dark resinous gum, to hold on the bark. (Cf. I, in which there was 'pitch', possibly to repair an ancient break.)

The covering is normally of bark, which in the Tutʿankhamūn bows is applied in large pieces (not in small rectangles, as in H). The only anomaly among the Tutʿankhamūn bows is the 'Bow of Honour' (4), completely covered with sheet gold.

SECTION (see Plate XIV)

More recent composite bows are consistent in structure. The ancient Egyptian ones are more varied. Several features distinguish them from later examples, but even these are not invariable.

Frequently, wooden lateral strips overlap the core, to provide a channel for the sinew backing or horn facing (A, C, D, G, H, I, 2, 7, 12, 14, 17; probably 15, 16, 18); but these side-strips were sometimes omitted, to produce a simpler section (B, F, 13 (?), 21; probably also 22–8).

Occasionally, there is horn backing as well as horn facing (A, C, H, I (?)); quite commonly, however, there is no horn backing (B, D, F, G, 14, 17, 29; probably 15, 16, 18). Possibly some bows from the tomb have sinew backing and sinew facing (21; cf. also 22–8).

[1] H. J. Plenderleith, *The Conservation of Antiquities and Works of Art* (London, 1956), p. 47.

Especially curious is the structure of **29**, with its lamellae of wood and sinew (or possibly horn) placed parallel to the lines of stress rather than across them.

These variations are roughly contemporary; they all occur in Eighteenth Dynasty specimens. They demonstrate conclusively that morphological variations are not chronological criteria.

## FUNCTIONAL DIFFERENTIATION OF THE PARTS OF THE BOW

The shaped grip and the flattened arm, refinements once thought to be later developments, occurred in ancient Egypt. The grip was occasionally reinforced with an additional layer of bark or thin wood (**D, I**). Frequently, the grip, though no wider than the lower part of the limbs, was thickened to be somewhat deeper than the limbs (**G, I, 6, 7, 8, 9, 10**). More sophisticated, a few examples are now seen to have a contracted grip, with broadened, often flattened, arms (**1**, not surprisingly; also **4, 17, 29**). The arm was likewise flattened in several other examples in which the section of the grip is unknown (**19, 21**).

Later composite bows regularly have a keel along the back; perhaps by way of foreshadowing this, a few Egyptian examples have a keel—but along the belly (**D, H, 14, 19** [rounded], **21, 29**; probably **27, 28**).

## NOCKS (see Plate xv)

Bows from other sources reveal that, at about 0·01 or 0·02 from the end of the bow, the wooden core was often bent further in the reflex direction (**A, C, H**; probably, to judge from the photograph, **I**; but not **G**). The Tutꜥankhamūn bows are too well preserved to confirm this detail, but the profiles suggest that here too the core is bent at the tip. They also show clearly how the exterior constituents were shaped. Towards the tip, the upper arm, which was normally flattened, swelled out to produce a projecting collar around the stave, about 0·01 from the tip; this would prevent the string from riding down the stave. The collar is nearly round in section (the two diameters are equal in **5, 6, 7, 8, 10**). Its plane is not perpendicular to the line of the arm, but is usually—not invariably—higher on the back.

Above the collar was a circumferent groove, deepest on the back, to lodge the string; on the face below the collar was a short vertical groove running along the stave, to prevent the string from slipping sideways and twisting the bow. It extended a mere 0·015 from the tip on the sole example for which measurements are given (**9**). This groove is mentioned in the notes on only four bows (**5, 7, 9, 10**); that it was not exceptional is indicated by Mace's comment on one (**10**), 'groove as usual'.

The knob beyond the nock varies in shape; sometimes the actual tip is flattened, sometimes it is rounded but set off by an angle, sometimes it is worked in a continuous curve.

## STRINGS

Bowstrings occasionally survive,[1] almost invariably of gut (**E**, intact when found; **G**, now lost; possibly decorative or structural binding). Two of Tutꜥankhamūn's composite bows had bits of bowstring adhering to the nock (**15, 17**). Several other fragments of bowstrings (Obj. no. 370 *mm*)

---

[1] Wolf, *Bewaffnung*, p. 48; LUCAS-HARRIS, pp. 29–30—both with references.

were found in the box, Obj. no. 370, which contained, *inter alia*, seven composite bows (**14–20**)—but no self bows. It seems likely that the string fragments came from composite bows in the box. All are four-strand twisted gut (cf. CARTER–MACE, III, p. 138), of varying thicknesses: 0·002, 0·0035, 0·0045.[1] Photograph: Plate XIII, top.

The manner in which the string was fixed to the bow is not clear. Presumably it was fastened to one end by a permanent knot. On self bows the string was attached by ten or twelve twists around the stave at each end, secured by one or more hitches at one end;[2] but this type of attachment, which necessarily covers much of the tip, is evidently not feasible for the grooved nock of the composite bows. An eye of some sort seems required.

The only bowstring knot drawn by Carter is one of the loose fragments mentioned above. It is a simple eye splice; the twisted gut was unlaid, its strands were looped around and passed through the unlaid portion, and knotted about the cord. Photograph: Plate XIII, bottom.

## DECORATION

The bark covering of other ancient Egyptian composite bows was decorated (**B** (?), **E**, **F**, **G** (?), **J**); but the most elaborate bows in the Tutʿankhamūn collection (**4, 9, 27, 28**) are far more ornate than any other. The only comparable example is the other royal bow (**F**). The Berlin bow (**G**) may have borne similar adornment, now vanished; the tips for some 0·28 preserve the impressions of extensive bindings. At the other extreme a few bows of Tutʿankhamūn are altogether undecorated (**17 18** (?), **20**).

Apart from these extremes, the decoration usually occurs in one or more circumferent zones. As a rule the grip is undecorated; sometimes it bears bands of contrasting colour (**7, 12, 16**, J.E. 61529, **E, J**; the last has bands of metopes).

Often there is a zone of decoration beside the grip (**1, 5** [cartouches], **6, 7, 8, 15, 16, 25, 26, 29**; **B**—traces of impressions only). Sometimes there is a zone at mid arm (**2** [titularies], **3** [cartouches], **11** [plain dark], **12** [banded], **13** [plain dark], **14** [gold], **15** [cartouches], **16** [cartouches]). Frequently there is a zone at or near the tip (**1, 2, 3** [cartouches], **5, 6, 7, 8, 10** [plain dark], **11** [plain dark], **12, 15** [cartouches], **16, 19** [plain dark], **21** [plain dark], **22** (?), **23** (?), **24, 25, 26, J**).

Twenty-three of the Tutʿankhamūn bows have an elongated rectangular panel on the face of the arm;[3] usually dark in colour, occasionally light (one of each pair of arms in **5**; one arm of **26**). This panel is often inscribed with hieroglyphs (**1, 2, 3, 5, 6, 7, 8, 9, 10, 11, 12, 13** (?), **15, 19**—all the longer inscriptions); by way of contrast, the bow of Amenophis II was inscribed on both the back and the face. Sometimes, especially in short bows, the panel is left plain (**21, 23** (?), **26, 28**, and J.E. 61540); sometimes it is decorated (**16**, overlapping zigzag; **22**, gilt pattern [of stars]; **24**, 'bark decoration'; **27**, lozenge chequerboard).

---

[1] LUCAS–HARRIS, pp. 29–30, says 0·0015 to 0·0035; also that one example of a linen bowstring was found.

[2] e.g. H. E. Winlock, *The Slain Soldiers of Neb-ḥepet-Rēʿ Mentu-ḥotpe*, (New York, 1945), p. 10, fig. 2.

[3] Carter's notes are not immediately clear here, but comparison of the phrasing of the descriptions with the photographs in most instances confirms that the panel was in fact on the face; see above, p. 4, n. 1. Some grounds for doubt remain for **13**; Mace, changing his usual terminology, places the panel on the 'back'. It seems likely that this too is an error for 'face'.

# HISTORICAL COMMENTARY

## SUMMARY

Anthropologists distinguish two chief varieties of bow. One is the 'self' bow, a simple wooden stave; this is the earlier type, and in the historical period it is still typical of Africa and Western Europe. The other is the 'composite' bow, made up of strips of various materials laminated together; this more sophisticated type developed in Asia, and at an early date supplanted the older type throughout the continent.[1]

In Egypt of the Old and Middle Kingdoms, the native African self bow was current. During the Second Intermediate Period, the composite bow was introduced, no doubt from Asia; a superior weapon, it was adopted with enthusiasm, and is well attested under the great pharaohs of the New Kingdom (c. 1570–1165 B.C.). They used it regularly, and boasted of their facility with it. After Ramesses III, it fell into eclipse; a single specimen is doubtfully ascribed to the Twenty-sixth Dynasty.

The ancient Egyptian composite bow had its own distinctive features which set it apart from later bows. Extant specimens regularly have a curious inward bend at the grip, which produces a double-curved profile, not unlike a common Egyptian type of wooden bow (see Plates III, XI). The resemblance is superficial, for in stringing the tips were bent back in the opposite direction; like all composite bows, they were 'reflexed'. When strung, the 'inward bend' became an external angle, and the profile became triangular; it is regularly so depicted in Egyptian art of the New Kingdom.[2]

[1] H. Balfour, 'On the Structure and Affinities of the Composite Bow', *JRAI*, 19 (1889/90), pp. 220–50; C. J. Longman, in C. J. Longman and Col. H. Walrond, *Archery* (Badminton Library of Sports and Pastimes, London, 1894), pp. 23–57, with map at end. The use of the term 'composite' for such bows is widespread, but by no means universal. They are sometimes called 'compound', as, for example, in Carter's notes; cf. CARTER–MACE, III, p. 138 *et passim*. To complicate matters further, some authorities distinguish between 'composite' and 'compound' bows; see D. Forde, in C. Singer, E. J. Holmyard, and A. R. Hall, *A History of Technology*, I (Oxford, 1954), p. 162.

[2] e.g. Karnak, eighth pylon (Amenophis II): Lepsius, *Denkmaeler*, III, pl. 61 (PORTER–MOSS, II, pp. 57–8 [44]); limestone stela from Thebes (Amenophis III): W. M. F. Petrie, *Six Temples at Thebes* (London, 1897), pl. 10 (PORTER–MOSS, II, p. 159); north outer wall of great temple at Karnak (Sethos I): Lepsius, *Denkmaeler*, III, pls. 126b, 127b, 128a, 130b (PORTER–MOSS, II, pp. 20 [55], 20 [58], 21 [57], 22 [63]); great temple at Abû Simbel (Ramesses II): Wreszinski, *Atlas*, II, pl. 181 (PORTER–MOSS, VII, p. 103 [39–40] third scene); Medînet Habu (Ramesses III): OIC Epigr. Survey (H. H. Nelson), *Medinet Habu*, I (Chicago, 1930), pl. 31; II (Chicago, 1932), pls. 93, 98, 117 = 130, 120, 121, 122.

On the angular bow, see H. Balfour, 'On a Remarkable Ancient Bow and Arrows believed to be of Assyrian Origin', *JRAI*, 26 (1896/7), pp. 210–20; F. E. Brown, 'A Recently Discovered Compound Bow', *SemKond*, 9 (1937), pp. 1–10; G. Brunton, 'Syrian Connections of a Composite Bow', *ASAE*, 38 (1938), pp. 251–2; C. J. Longman, 'The Bows of the Ancient Assyrians and Egyptians', *JRAI*, 24 (1894/5), pp. 49–57; F. von Luschan, 'Ueber einen zusammengesetzten Bogen aus der Zeit Rhamses II', *Verh. Berl. Anthrop. Gesellsch.*, Beibl. to *ZfE*, 25 (1893), pp. 266–71; W. McLeod, 'An unpublished Egyptian Composite Bow in the Brooklyn Museum', *AJA*, 62 (1958), pp. 397–401; repr. *JSA-A*, 3 (1960), pp. 11–17; 'Egyptian Composite Bows in New York', *AJA*, 66 (1962), pp. 13–19; 'Tutankhamen's Composite Bows (from Howard Carter's Unpublished Notes)', *JSA-A*, 7 (1964), pp. 16–19; H. Mebert, 'Der Assyrische Angularbogen als Kriegs- und Jagdwaffe', *Ztschr. f. hist. Waff. u. Kostümk.*, 15 (1937/9), pp. 96–100; E. Robinson, 'The Egyptian Composite Bow', *Archery* (Los Angeles, National Field Archery Association), 23.4 (April, 1951), pp. 4–5; G. A. Wainwright, 'Ancient Survivals in Modern Africa', *Bull. Soc. sultanieh de géog.*, 9 (1919), pp. 109–15, 193–7.

When the bow was drawn, the angle almost disappeared, and the bow exhibited a continuous sweeping curve extending through the grip.[1] Beyond any question this variety of weapon was introduced from Asia; and it lingered on in the homeland, for it occurs in Hittite and Mesopotamian art on and off until the Persian advent.[2]

Of the ten other ancient Egyptian composite bows, six (**A–F**) are earlier than those from the tomb (at least five of them Eighteenth Dynasty), and only one (**G**) is certainly later (Nineteenth Dynasty). Of the bows in the present catalogue, four bear the nomen of Tutᶜankhaten (**1, 6, 7, 8**), and ten that of Tutᶜankhamūn (**2, 3, 5, 9, 10, 11, 12, 13, 15, 19**). It might be assumed that this distinction is chronological; it must, however, be noted that certain other objects bear both nomina simultaneously.[3]

### PLACE OF MANUFACTURE

The composite bow being of Asiatic inspiration, individual bows of this type from Egypt have been taken for imports. Thus the Berlin bow (**G**), according to von Luschan, belonged to either a Hittite captive or an Asiatic mercenary. In the Oxford bow (**H**), Balfour recognized a trophy from the Assyrian invasion. Brunton pointed out that a bow in Cairo (**E**) had been buried with one Se-aa, a name which seems to be Syrian.

As if in confirmation, botanical analysis disclosed that the wood or bark in certain of the bows was alien to Egypt, but native to Western Asia (ash, birch, and possibly cherry).[4] Recently Helck has asserted that birch bark can be used only in a fresh state, and that its presence on bows attests that they were manufactured in Asia and imported into Egypt.[5]

As a matter of fact, large trees have always been so scarce in Egypt that even in antiquity imported wood was used for making all sorts of goods, among them mummy cases, chariots, and even the shrines from the burial chambers of Tutᶜankhamūn.[6] Yet no one has tried to give these objects a foreign provenience. On the question of birch bark, I have been privileged to consult Dr. J. J. Balatinecz, of the Faculty of Forestry in the University of Toronto. He states that birch bark retains its pliability for a considerable time, and that even after drying it can be softened by moisture; Helck's assertion, it seems, is untrue, and his inference unjustified. In sum, there is no real reason to believe that any Egyptian composite bow was made outside Egypt.

---

[1] Thus, for example, Tutᶜankhamūn's gold fan depicting his ostrich hunt (Obj. no. 242); on the front, the bow is drawn; on the back, it is angular: CARTER–MACE, II, pl. 62; *Treasure*, pls. 24, 25; *Toutankhamon*, pl. 20. So, too, the reliefs on the chariot of Tuthmosis IV: H. Carter and P. E. Newberry, *The Tomb of Thoutmôsis IV* (Westminster, 1904), pl. 11. Likewise, in Assyrian art: R. D. Barnett and N. Falkner, *The Sculptures of Aššur-naṣir-apli II* (London, 1962), pl. 72.

[2] Late Hittite reliefs: e.g. H. T. Bossert, *Altanatolien* (Berlin, 1942), figs. 775, 817; Assyrian art: e.g. J. B. Pritchard, *The Ancient Near East in Pictures Relating to the Old Testament* (Princeton, 1954), figs. 351, 371, 626; cf. also the Hasanlu bowl: *Expedition*, 1. 3 (1959), p. 18, bottom. On its extinction, see F. E. Brown, *SemKond*, 9 (1937), p. 7; H. Mebert, *Ztschr. f. hist. Waff. u. Kostümk.*, 15 (1937/9), p. 100.

[3] e.g. the 'ecclesiastical' throne (Obj. no. 351), found in the Annexe; it bears Amūn and Aten cartouches, both

apparently being original: CARTER–MACE, III, p. 112; *Treasure*, pl. 60. The secular throne (Obj. no. 91), from the Antechamber, also has both cartouches, but the Amūn cartouches are almost certainly substitutions: CARTER–MACE, I, p. 118; *Treasure*, p. 17.

[4] Ash (*Fraxinus* sp., probably not *F. ornus*), **16**; flowering or manna ash (*F. ornus*), see above, p. 31; European white birch (*Betula pendula* Roth, *B. verrucosa* Ehrh., *B. alba* L. in part), **A, B, C, D**; these identifications are by botanical experts. Archaeologists' identifications include cherry bark (**I, 14, 16, 19**) and birch bark (**G, H, 15, 17, 19, 21, 23, 29**); on the authority of such guesses, see LUCAS–HARRIS, pp. 454–5.

[5] H. W. Helck, *Die Beziehungen Ägyptens zu Vorderasien*, p. 545. This notion apparently goes back to I. Rosellini, as quoted by H. Schäfer, 'Armenisches Holz in altägyptischen Wagnereien', *Sitz. Berlin* (Phil.-Hist.), 1931, pp. 731, 733.

[6] List in LUCAS–HARRIS, pp. 429–39.

The tombs of Puimrēᶜ and Menkheperrēᶜsonb at Thebes establish clearly that angular bows were manufactured in the temple-workshops of the temple of Amūn in the time of Tuthmosis III. A funeral stela in the Louvre, of an 'overseer of the bowyer-craftsmen' in a factory of the later Eighteenth Dynasty, also shows angular bows being made.[1] In the light of all this, are we to see Western Asia as the source of Tutᶜankhamūn's composite bows? *Credat Iudaeus Apella, non ego.*[2]

## PERFORMANCE

The pharaohs of the Egyptian New Kingdom sought renown as archers, and with the new and powerful composite bow they chalked up some spectacular achievements. One regular feat was to shoot at copper ingots, which their arrows were said to transpierce; this is recorded of Tuthmosis III, Amenophis II, Tuthmosis IV, Ay, and Ramesses II.[3] There is no direct testimony as to the range of the ancient Egyptian composite bow. Ancient bows are too fragile to test, and their power can only be inferred.

The English yew long-bow was effective up to 220 metres, and could cast a flight arrow as far as 265 metres; but it was the finest self bow ever devised, and probably far surpassed any wooden bow of the ancients. A series of tests of weapons from anthropological collections suggests that wooden bows, not unlike the native Egyptian one, might attain a maximum range of 155–90 metres. A good composite bow is more powerful than a good self bow.[4]

Modern replicas of angular bows have been made, several by the German bowyer Hellmut Mebert, of Stuttgart, but details of their manufacture or performance are not available. Another was made by the American anthropologist Saxton Pope; its profile was of the Turkish type, but the section was modelled after that of the Berlin bow (**G**). On several tries it cast flight arrows a distance of 230–60 metres.[5] The oldest composite bows for which we have explicit data, those current in the classical world, were effective up to a distance of more than 175 metres, but not so far as 350 metres.[6]

On this slender testimony we may perhaps hazard a guess that the best of the Tutᶜankhamūn bows fell not far short of later composite bows in performance.

[1] Tombs 39, 86; see PORTER–MOSS, I. i², pp. 71 [3], 177 [5]; pictures: Wreszinski, *Atlas*, I, pls. 152, 80–1; A. Moret, 'Stèle de la XVIIIᵉ dynastie représentant une fabrique d'arcs', *RA* ser. 3, 34 (1899), pp. 231–9.

[2] This question is discussed more fully in a paper entitled 'Were Egyptian Composite Bows made in Asia?', to appear in *JSA-A*, 12 (1969).

[3] *Urk.* IV. 1245. 1–11 (Armant stela); 1280.9–1281.5 (Gîza stela); 1304.3–4 (Memphis stela); 1321–2 (granite block from third pylon of the great temple at Karnak, with text and relief); 1541.10 (Sphinx stela: PORTER–MOSS, III, p. 8); T. M. Davis, *The Tombs of Harmhabi and Touatânkhamanou* (London, 1912), p. 127 (gold-leaf: PORTER–MOSS, I. ii², p. 588); *University of Pennsylvania Museum Journal*, 20 (1929), p. 55 (cylinder seal from Bethshan: PORTER–MOSS, VII, p. 379). Experiments suggest that an arrow readily penetrates chain mail or plate armour, if it hits squarely. Against this background, the pharaonic copper-piercing projectiles are too impressive to command credence; see *AJA*, 66 (1962), p. 15; W. F. Paterson, *JESHO*, 9 (1966), p. 86. On the sporting tradition, see H. Schäfer,

'König Amenophis II als Meisterschütz', *OLZ*, 32 (1929), cols. 233–44; 'Weiteres zum Bogenschiessen im alten Aegypten', *OLZ*, 34 (1931), cols. 89–96; N. de G. Davies, 'The King as Sportsman', *BMMA*, 30 (1935), *Egyptian Exped. 1934–1935*, pp. 49–53; B. van de Walle, 'Les rois sportifs de l'ancienne Égypte', *Cd'E*, 13 (1938), pp. 234–57; A. de Buck, 'Een sportief egyptisch Koning', *JEOL*, 2 (1939/42), pp. 9–14; C. Desroches-Noblecourt, 'Un petit monument commémoratif du roi athlète', *Rd'E*, 7 (1950), pp. 37–46; J. A. Wilson, *The Burden of Egypt* (Chicago, 1951) (reprinted as *The Culture of Ancient Egypt*), pp. 195–201; and especially W. C. Hayes, 'The Sporting Tradition', *CAH*², 2, ch. 9, § 5 (= fasc. 10 [1962], pt. 1, pp. 23–8).

[4] 'The Range of the Ancient Bow', *Phoenix*, 19 (1965), pp. 1–14, especially 13–14.

[5] S. T. Pope, *Bows and Arrows* (Berkeley and Los Angeles, 1962): reprint of 'A Study of Bows and Arrows', *U. Cal. Pub. in Am. Arch. and Ethn.*, 13.9 (1923, revised 1930), pp. 30–1.

[6] *Phoenix*, 19 (1965), p. 8.

# NOTES TO THE PLATES

Plate I. Close-up of objects in the north-west corner of the Antechamber, showing the group of bows and staves (Obj. no. 48) *in situ* on the bed upon the lion-headed couch.

MMA neg. TAA 16 = GI neg. 21. *Photograph by Harry Burton. Griffith Institute.*

Plate II. The group of bows and staves (Obj. no 48), including composite bows **1–10** in their original linen wrappings, still in position upon the bed after removal from the couch.

MMA neg. TAA 152 = GI neg. 23. *Photograph by Harry Burton. Griffith Institute.*

Plate III. Obj. no. 77 *a* (self bow); composite bows **5, 1, 7, 9, 4** (Obj. nos. 48 *i* (1), 48 *f*, 48 *j* (1), 48 *k* (1), 48 *h*).

Complete, from side. The face of the composite bows is towards the top of the picture, the back of the self bow.

MMA neg. TAA 155 = GI neg. 484 (*ILN*, 20 October 1928, p. 712).

*Photograph by Harry Burton. Griffith Institute.*

Plate IV. Composite bows **4, 1, 5** (Obj. nos. 48 *h*, 48 *f*, 48 *i* (1)).

Grip and lower arm, from face; the grip is at the bottom of the picture.

MMA neg. TAA 153 = GI neg. 485 (Carter–Mace, I, pl. 76).

*Photograph by Harry Burton. Griffith Institute.*

Plate V. Composite bows **4, 1, 5** (Obj. nos. 48 *h*, 48 *f*, 48 *i* (1)).

Tip, from side. The back is towards the top of the picture. The strings tied to the mid upper arm of the top bow, the upper arm of the middle bow, and the nock of the bottom bow are modern.

MMA neg. TAA 154 = GI neg. 487. *Photograph by Harry Burton. Griffith Institute.*

Plate VI. Composite bows **9, 7, 4** (Obj. nos. 48 *k* (1), 48 *j* (1), 48 *h*).

Grip and lower arm, from back; the grip is at the bottom of the picture.

MMA neg. TAA 157 = GI neg. 488. *Photograph by Harry Burton. Griffith Institute.*

Plate VII. Composite bows **7, 9, 4** (Obj. nos. 48 *j* (1), 48 *k* (1), 48 *h*).

Tip, from side. The back is towards the top of the picture.

MMA neg. TAA 156 = GI neg. 486 (Carter–Mace, I, pl. 77).

*Photograph by Harry Burton. Griffith Institute.*

Plate VIII. Composite bows **17, 16, 15, 14** (Obj. nos. 370 *ii*, 370 *hh*, 370 *gg*, 370 *ff*).

Centre of bow, grip and lower arms, from side. The back is towards the top of the picture.

MMA neg. TAA 1142. *Photograph by Harry Burton. The Metropolitan Museum of Art.*

Plate IX. Composite bows **14, 15, 16, 17** (Obj. nos. 370 *ff*, 370 *gg*, 370 *hh*, 370 *ii*).

Centre of bow, grip and lower arms, from face.

MMA neg. TAA 158 = GI neg. 1209. *Photograph by Harry Burton. Griffith Institute.*

Plate x. Composite bows **17, 16, 15, 14** (Obj. nos. 370 *ii*, 370 *hh*, 370 *gg*, 370 *ff*).

Tip, from side. The back is towards the top of the picture.

MMA neg. TAA 1141.                          *Photograph by Harry Burton. The Metropolitan Museum of Art.*

Plate xi. Composite bows **21, 26, 27, 28, 29** (Obj. nos. 596 *k*, 596 *p*, 596 *q*, 596 *r*, 596 *s*); Obj. no. 596 *t* (self bow).

Complete, from side. The face of the composite bows is towards the top of the picture, the back of the self bow.

MMA neg. TAA 159 = GI neg. 1208 (*ILN*, 12 October 1929, p. 626).
                                           *Photograph by Harry Burton. Griffith Institute.*

Plate xii. Composite bows **29, 27, 28** (Obj. nos. 596 *s*, 596 *q*, 596 *r*).

Grip and lower arm, from face. The grip is towards the bottom of the picture.

MMA neg. TAA 160 (*JSA-A*, 7 [1964], p. 18).
                                           *Photograph by Harry Burton. The Metropolitan Museum of Art.*

Plate xiii.

top: Fragments of bowstrings (Obj. no. 370 *mm*) found in the box containing composite bows **14–20**.

MMA neg. TAA 169 = GI neg. 1207.            *Photograph by Harry Burton. Griffith Institute.*

bottom: Carter's record card for the fragments, with sketch of knot.

Plate xiv. Cross-sections of ancient Egyptian composite bows. Unless otherwise stated, sections are taken at or near the grip, with the back uppermost; actual size. Hatching = wood (but in the Tutʿankhamūn bows possibly also horn; see above, p. 32); cross-hatching = wood, or possibly horn; close stippling = sinew; open stippling = gelatinous substance (probably hydrolysed sinew; possibly hydrolysed horn); black = horn.

A. New York, MMA, Acc. no. 28. 9. 9; after *AJA*, 66 (1962), pl. 11, fig. 1*a*.

B. New York, MMA, Acc. no. 25. 3. 303$^1$; after *AJA*, 66 (1962), pl. 11, fig. 1*b*.

C. New York, MMA, Acc. no. 25. 3. 303$^2$; after *AJA*, 66 (1962), pl. 11, fig. 1*c*.

D. New York, MMA, Acc. no. 25. 3. 304; after *AJA*, 66 (1962), pl. 11, fig. 1*d*.

E. Cairo, Eg. Mus., J.E. 31389; no scale; tentatively reconstructed on basis of published description.

F. Cairo, Eg. Mus., J.E. 32612; no scale; tentatively reconstructed on basis of published descriptions.

G. Berlin, Staatliche Mus., Aeg. Abt., Inv. nr. 4712; after *AJA*, 62 (1958), pl. 108, fig. 8*b*.

H. Oxford, Pitt Rivers Mus. (Balfour's bow); section in mid arm; after *AJA*, 62 (1958), pl. 108, fig. 8*a*.

I. New York, Brooklyn Mus., Acc. no. 37. 1835E; after *AJA*, 62 (1958), pl. 109, fig. 6. 1.

14. Tutʿankhamūn Tomb, Obj. no. 370 *ff*; lower arm; after a measured section by Carter.

17*a*, 17*b*. Tutʿankhamūn Tomb, Obj. no. 370 *ii*; grip and lower arm; no scale; after sketches by Carter.

19. Tutʿankhamūn Tomb, Obj. no. 370 *kk*; probably arm; no scale; after a sketch by Carter; no indication of structure.

21. Tutʿankhamūn Tomb, Obj. no. 596 *k*; probably arm; no scale; after a sketch by Carter.

29. Tutʿankhamūn Tomb, Obj. no. 596 *s*; probably arm; no scale; after a sketch by Carter.

Plate xv. Nocks of ancient Egyptian composite bows. Unless otherwise stated, the tips are seen from the side, with the back to the left; approximately one-half actual size.

A. New York, MMA, Acc. no. 28. 9. 9; schematic reconstruction: one tip as preserved (cross-hatched), with tentative outline of the original profile, reconstructed on the basis of the Tutꜥankhamūn bows.

1. Tutꜥankhamūn Tomb, Obj. no. 48 *f*; after Burton's photograph, Plate v.

2. Tutꜥankhamūn Tomb, Obj. no. 48 *g* (1); after a sketch by Mace.

3. Tutꜥankhamūn Tomb, Obj. no. 48 *g* (2); after a sketch by Mace.

4. Tutꜥankhamūn Tomb, Obj. no. 48 *h*; after Burton's photograph, Plate v.

5. Tutꜥankhamūn Tomb, Obj. no. 48 *i* (1); after Burton's photograph, Plate v.

7. Tutꜥankhamūn Tomb, Obj. no. 48 *j* (1); after Burton's photograph, Plate vii.

9. Tutꜥankhamūn Tomb, Obj. no. 48 *k* (1); after Burton's photograph, Plate vii.

11. Tutꜥankhamūn Tomb, Obj. no. 77 *b*; after a sketch by Mace.

13. Tutꜥankhamūn Tomb, Obj. no. 153; after a sketch by Mace.

14*a*. Tutꜥankhamūn Tomb, Obj. no. 370 *ff*; from face; after a sketch by Carter.

14*b*. Tutꜥankhamūn Tomb, Obj. no. 370 *ff*; after Burton's photograph, Plate x.

15. Tutꜥankhamūn Tomb, Obj. no. 370 *gg*; after Burton's photograph, Plate x.

16. Tutꜥankhamūn Tomb, Obj. no. 370 *hh*; after Burton's photograph, Plate x.

17. Tutꜥankhamūn Tomb, Obj. no. 370 *ii*; after Burton's photograph, Plate x.

21. Tutꜥankhamūn Tomb, Obj. no. 596 *k*; after a sketch by Carter.

Plate xvi. Inscriptions on bows **1–3** (Obj. nos. 48 *f*, 48 *g* (1), 48 *g* (2)).

Plate xvii. Inscriptions on bows **4–7** (Obj. nos. 48 *h*, 48 *i* (1), 48 *i* (2), 48 *j* (1)).

Plate xviii. Inscriptions on bows **8–11** (Obj. nos. 48 *j* (2), 48 *k* (1), 48 *k* (2), 77 *b*).

Plate xix. Inscriptions on bows **12–19** (Obj. nos. 135 *z*, 153, 370 *gg*, 370 *kk*).

Plate xx.

*a*. Enlarged detail of the cartouche of Inscription 4. 1 (from Plate iv).

*b*. Enlarged detail of the cartouche of Inscription 4. 2 (from Plate iv).

*c*. Hand-copy (after G.T.M.) of the traces visible in the cartouche of Inscription 4. 1.

*d*. Hand-copy (after G.T.M.) of the traces visible in the cartouche of Inscription 4. 2.

*e*. Suggested restoration of the original cartouche of Inscription 4. 1.

*f*. Prenomen of Smenkhkarēꜥ on the knob of a box, Obj. no. 1 *k*: that on a strip from the same box is similar, but omits the final ⲓⲓⲓ.

*g*. Prenomen of Smenkhkarēꜥ (later usurped) on the knob of a box, Obj. no. 574: that on a strip on the same part of the box is similar.

*h*. Prenomen of Smenkhkarēꜥ on a bracelet, Obj. no. 620 (42): that on a second bracelet, Obj. no. 620 (41), is now partly illegible, but was apparently similar, with the signs facing in the reverse direction.

*i*. Prenomen of Smenkhkarēꜥ on finger rings from El-Amarna (after W. M. F. Petrie, *Tell el Amarna* [London, 1894], pl. 15, nos. 92, 93).

PLATE I

The Group of Bows and Staves including Composite Bows **1–10**, *in situ*
Photograph by Harry Burton. Griffith Institute

PLATE II

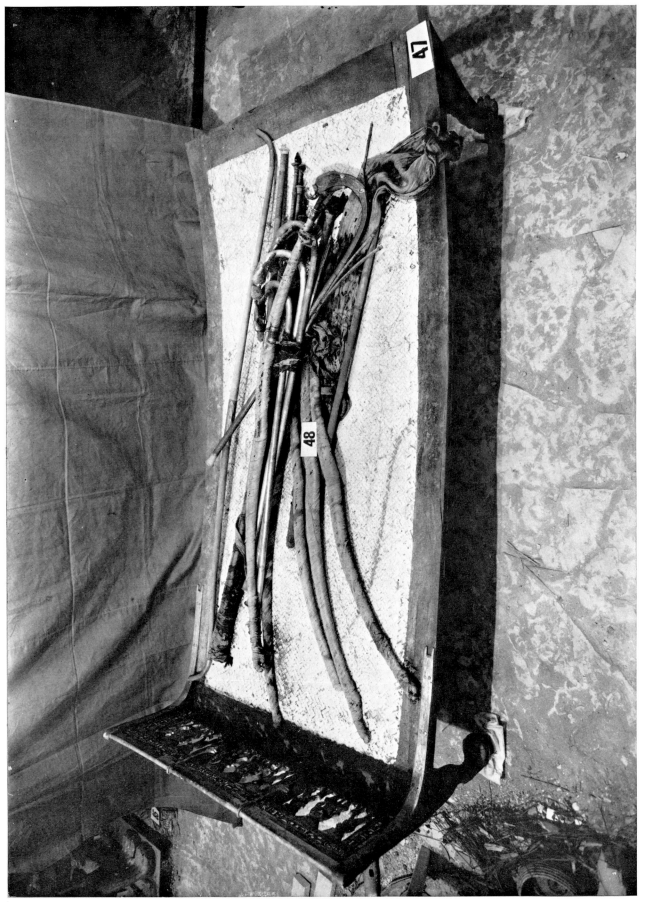

The Group of Bows and Staves including Composite Bows **1–10**, as found

PLATE III

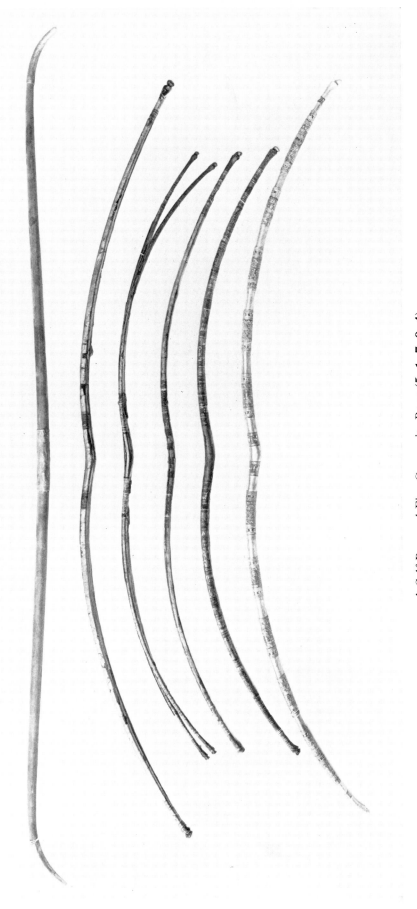

A Self Bow and Five Composite Bows (**5, 1, 7, 9, 4**)
Photograph by Harry Burton. Griffith Institute

PLATE IV

Composite Bows **4, 1, 5**
Photograph by Harry Burton. Griffith Institute

PLATE V

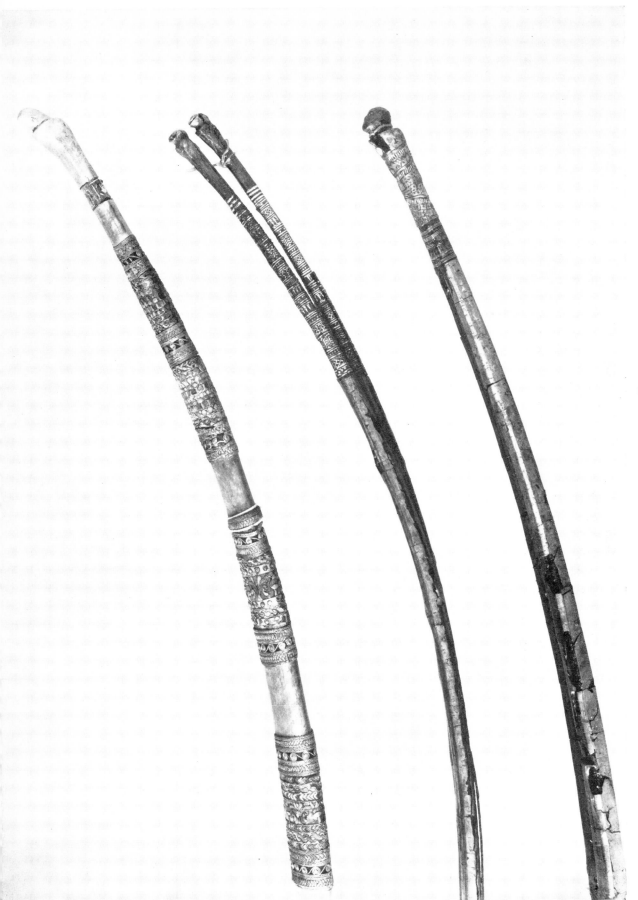

Composite Bows **4, 1, 5**
Photograph by Harry Burton. Griffith Institute

PLATE VI

Composite Bows **9, 7, 4**
Photograph by Harry Burton. Griffith Institute

PLATE VII

Composite Bows 7, 9, 4
Photograph by Harry Burton. Griffith Institute

PLATE VIII

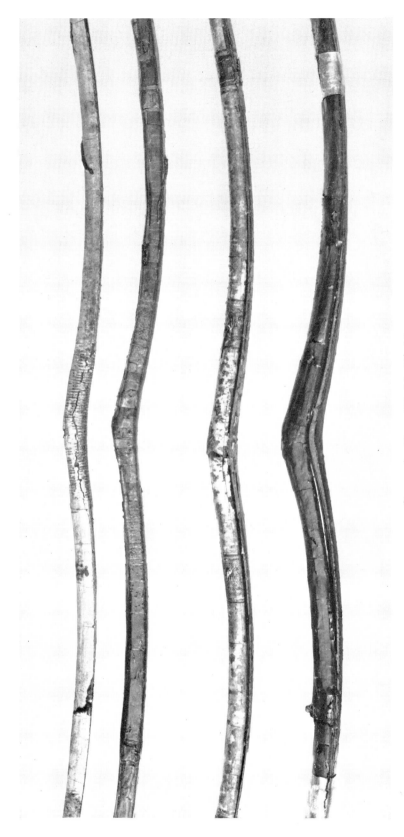

Composite Bows **17, 16, 15, 14**

Photograph by Harry Burton. The Metropolitan Museum of Art

PLATE IX

Composite Bows **14, 15, 16, 17**
Photograph by Harry Burton. Griffith Institute

PLATE X

Composite Bows **17, 16, 15, 14**
Photograph by Harry Burton. The Metropolitan Museum of Art

PLATE XI

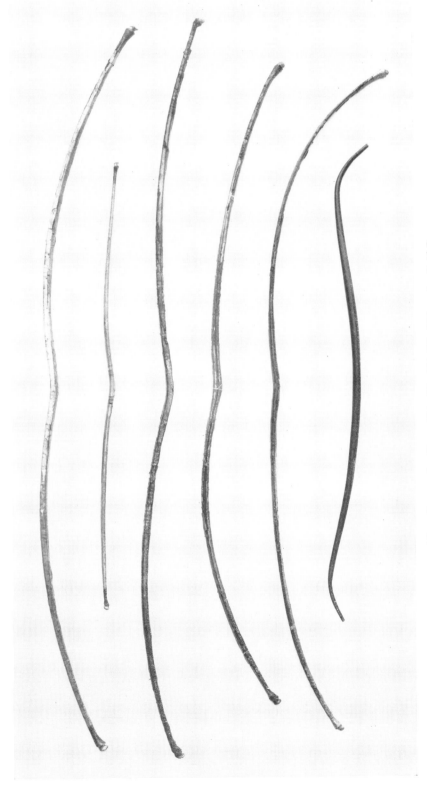

Five Composite Bows (**21, 26, 27, 28, 29**) and a Self Bow
Photograph by Harry Burton. Griffith Institute

PLATE XII

Composite Bows **29, 27, 28**
Photograph by Harry Burton. The Metropolitan Museum of Art

PLATE XIII

Fragments of Bowstrings
Photograph by Harry Burton. Griffith Institute

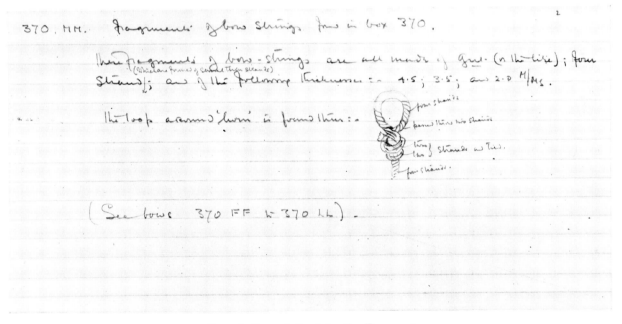

Carter's Record Card for the Fragments

PLATE XIV

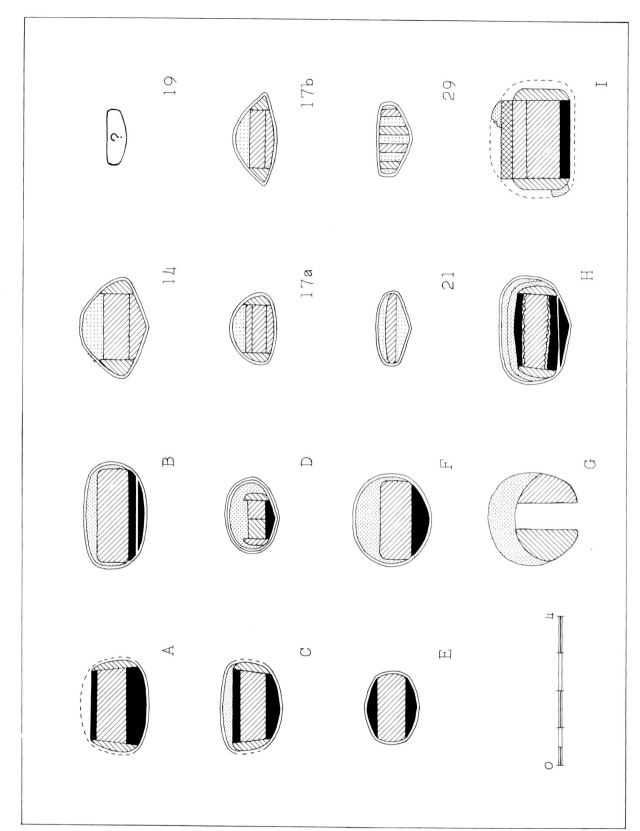

Cross-sections of Ancient Egyptian Composite Bows

PLATE XV

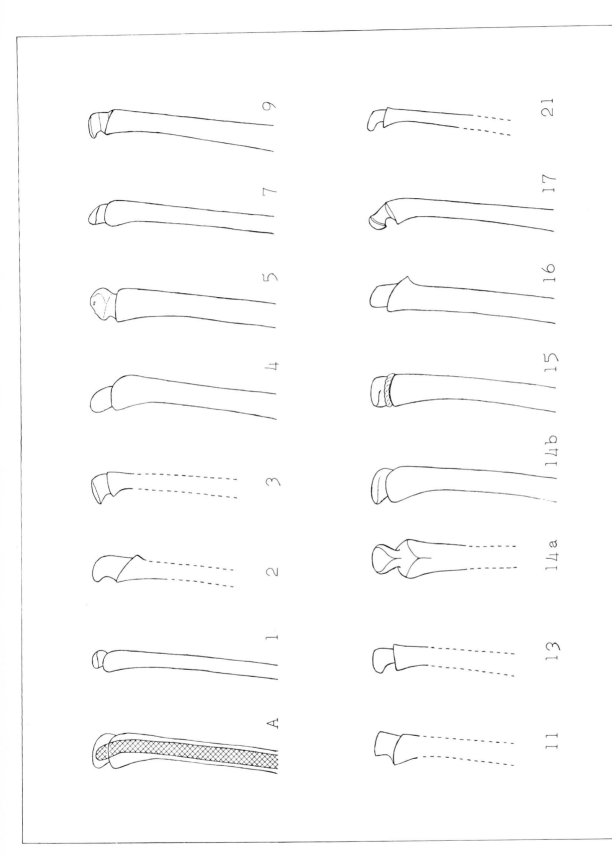

Nocks of Ancient Egyptian Composite Bows

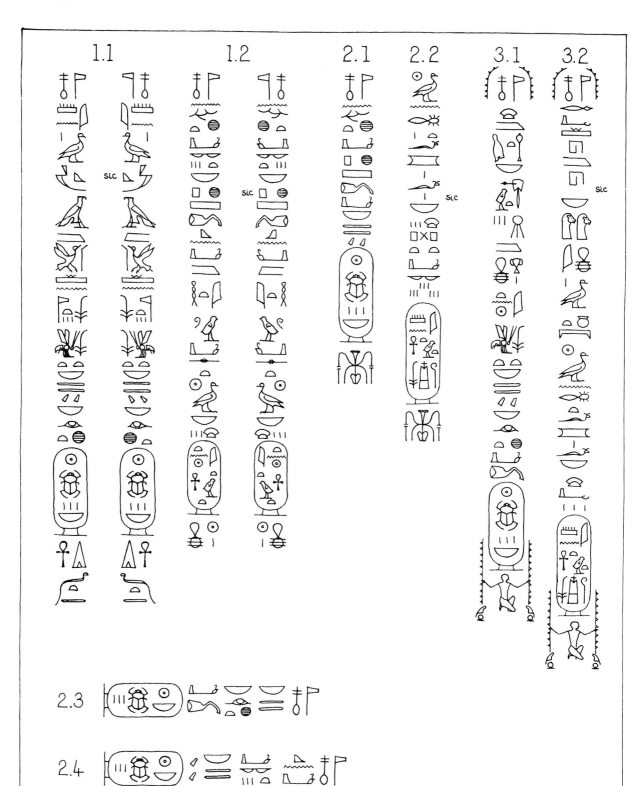

PLATE XVII

PLATE XVIII

PLATE XIX

PLATE XX

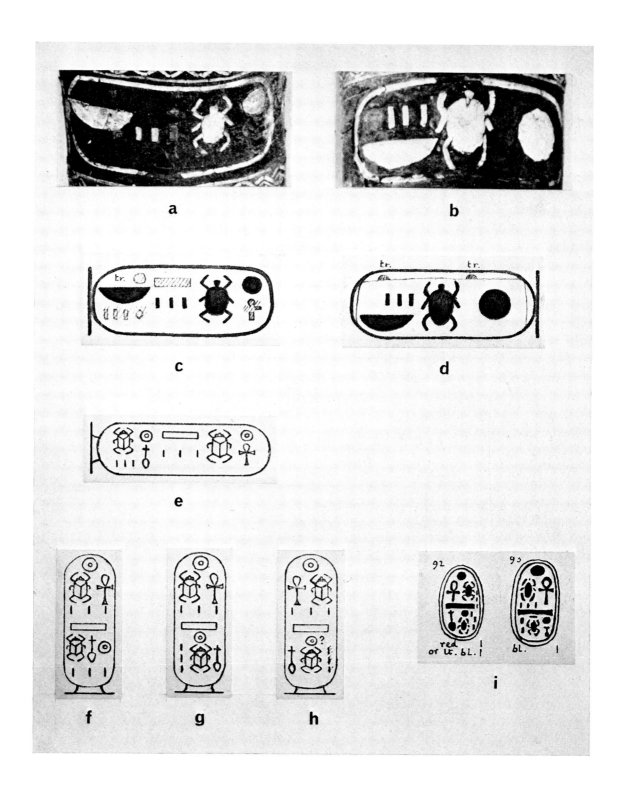

a

b

c

d

e

f

g

h

i